ENGLISH FOR ACADEMIC PURPOSES SERIES

General Editor: Vaughan James

GENERAL ENGINEERING

C M and D Johnson

Cassell

Cassell Publishers Ltd
Artillery House
Artillery Row
London
SW1P 1RT

First published 1988

British Library Cataloguing in Publication Data

Johnson, D. (David)
General engineering.—(English for
academic purposes).
Student's book
1. English language. For non-English
speaking students
I. Title II. Johnson, C.M. (Christine M.)
III. Series
428.2'4

ISBN 0 304 31520 6

A series designed and developed by Passim Ltd, Oxford, and Associates

Printed in England

General Engineering Teacher's Book 0 304 31521 4
Cassettes   0 304 31522 2

CONTENTS

INTRODUCTION

This course has three purposes. It is intended:
- to introduce you to the **contents** of General Engineering:
- to provide examples of authentic texts written in the **language** typical of the subject:
- to help you to practise the **skills** you will need in order to study the subject via English and to use it when you have learned it.

No knowledge of General Engineering is assumed, but if you work through the book carefully you will certainly learn a great deal about it. We do not set out to give comprehensive coverage, but the material does embrace most of the basic concepts. In this sense it is a basic textbook of General Engineering.

All the texts are taken from publications about General Engineering. They are not simplified for learners of English: the language you will encounter in them is exactly what you will meet in real life. We assume that you will have already taken a course of general English and are familiar with the main grammatical structures and much of the vocabulary of everyday use. There may be no such thing as General Engineering English, but there are a number of words and expressions commonly used in General Engineering contexts and there are a number of structures also in common use, and these have been isolated for you to practise. So in this sense, this is a textbook of English.

The most important aim of the course, however, is to help you to acquire and develop the skills you will need in order to learn your subject and, when you have finished the course, to use what you will have learned.

When you begin to study a new subject, you do so in two main ways: by **reading** and by **listening**. These are the major means of access to new knowledge and it is on these that we concentrate, via the **book** — for reading, and the **tapes** — for listening. In order to attack all these aims, we have divided each of the 15 units into 8 sections, closely related but each with a slightly different emphasis. Below we give a brief description of each section, so that at any point in any unit you will know exactly what you are expected to do and why you are doing it. The pattern is the same for all units.

A. UNDERSTANDING A PRINTED TEXT (1): In this section you are given a passage to read, usually including a diagram or table, to introduce the topic of the unit. You should first read it through, even if you do not understand it all, looking especially at the way it is set out in paragraphs, with side headings, marginal notes, captions, etc. This will give you a general idea of what it is about and how it is arranged. You will probably need to read it several times.

B. CHECK YOUR UNDERSTANDING: To help you to identify the most important points in the reading passage, a small number of questions are given, the answers to which you can look out for as you read. You could tackle them by jotting down a few notes and then turning your notes into complete answers, which your teacher will check. When you are clear about the general meaning of the passage, you can work through it in more detail with your dictionary. You should *always* have a dictionary handy and *never* be too proud (or too lazy!) to look things up.

C. INCREASE YOUR VOCABULARY: In this section you are asked to look at certain words which are used in the text, and there are several kinds of activity to help you remember them. Notice that they are not all new or technical terms; it is often familar words used in an unfamiliar way that will cause you trouble.

D. CHECK YOUR GRAMMAR: There are probably no new grammatical structures in the texts, but you may need reminding of some of them. The most important ones arising from the texts are revised and practised in this section.

E. UNDERSTANDING A LECTURE / H. UNDERSTANDING DISCOURSE: Sections A–D are all concerned with gaining access to new information through reading, but an important source of information is through listening — to lectures, talks, discussions, even simple conversations between fellow students — so sections E and H are both based on the recordings, to which you should listen (usually several times) before attempting to answer the questions or perform the activities given in your book. You will hear a variety of voices and accents, all speaking at the sort of speed that is customary in an English-speaking environment.

F. UNDERSTANDING A PRINTED TEXT (2) / G. CHECK YOUR UNDERSTANDING: These two sections are very similar to A and B, but the questions in section G are far more detailed and you will need to study the text very carefully in order to answer them.

   Although we hope that you will enjoy working through this course, we do not expect you to find it easy. At various times you will probably start wondering how much you have been learning — or your teacher will want to find out what progress you are making. So after Units 5 and 10 we have included progress checks (not tests!) so that you can get a fairly clear idea of this. By the time you have completed Unit 15, you will be ready for anything!

Some of the texts are written in American English, which has some differences from British English, especially in spelling (e.g. *Br.* vapour, *Am.* vapor). You might find it useful to keep a running list of such examples. Remember that they are equally acceptable, but you should avoid mixing them in a single piece of writing.

Vaughan James   Oxford, 1988

METALS

A. Understanding a printed text

This passage will give you some information about **metals, alloys and their uses**. Notice how it is divided into paragraphs and sections. Pay attention to the headings or notes in the margin.

Now look at the following questions:

1. What is the main advantage of metals?

2. Can plastics be recycled?
3. Which type of heat treatment makes metal softer and less brittle?
4. Why are Concorde's engine surrounds made of titanium alloys?

Read the passage to find the answers. Remember that you do not need to understand every word in order to do so.

Uses

Why does man use metals still so much today when there are other materials, especially plastics, which are available? A material is generally used because it offers the required strength, and other properties, at minimum cost. Appearance is also an important factor. The main advantage of metals is their strength and toughness. Concrete may be cheaper and is **5** often used in building, but even concrete depends on its core of steel for strength.

Plastics

Plastics are lighter and more corrosion-resistant, but they are not usually as strong. Another problem with plastics is what to do with them after use. Metal objects can often be broken down and the metals recycled; plastics **10** can only be dumped or burned.

Alloys

Not all metals are strong, however. Copper and aluminium, for example, are both fairly weak — but if they are mixed together, the result is an alloy called aluminium bronze, which is much stronger than either pure copper or pure aluminium. Alloying is an important method of obtaining whatever **15** special properties are required: strength, toughness, resistance to wear, magnetic properties, high electrical resistance or corrosion resistance.

Heat treatment

The properties of a metal can be further improved by use of heat treatment. Heat treatment is the term given to a number of different procedures in which the properties of metals and alloys are changed. It **20** usually consists of heating the metal or alloy to a selected temperature below its melting point and then cooling it at a certain rate to obtain those properties which are required. For example, hardening is used to make metals harder. Tempering makes them softer and less brittle. Annealing is carried out to make a metal soft so that it can be machined more easily. In **25** this way, metallic materials can be produced to meet every kind of engineering specification and requirement.

Special alloys

When Concorde was built, a material was needed which could withstand extreme aerodynamic conditions and would have a life of at least 45,000 flying hours. To achieve this, a special aluminium alloy was developed **30** which is tough and lightweight and is used in over 70% of Concorde's structure. Another 16% is made of high-strength steel, and titanium alloys are used in the engine surrounds to withstand temperatures of 4000 degrees centigrade.

Methods of extracting, producing and treating metals are being **35** developed all the time to meet engineering requirements. This means that there is an enormous variety of metals and metallic materials available from which to choose.

B. Check your understanding

Now read the text carefully, looking up anything you do not understand in a dictionary or reference book. While you read, look for the answers to these questions:

1. Put T or F in the boxes to indicate if the statements below are true or false according to the facts in the passage.
   - Concrete is a cheap building material. ☐
   - Plastics are more easily recycled than metals. ☐
   - Aluminium bronze is an example of an alloy. ☐
   - Pure copper is stronger than the alloys that are made by mixing copper with aluminium. ☐

- Tempering is a kind of heat treatment. ☐
- It is sometimes an advantage for a metal to be soft. ☐
- Concorde is built mainly of steel. ☐

2. Answer the following questions:
   - On line 3, which noun does the pronoun 'it' refer to?
   - On line 9, which nouns does the pronoun 'them' refer to?
   - On line 14, what does the word 'which' refer to?
   - On line 20, what does the pronoun 'it' refer to?
   - On line 22, which noun or nouns does the word 'its' refer to?
   - On line 22, does the word 'it' refer to the same noun as that at the beginning of the line?

C. Increase your vocabulary

1. Properties of materials

(a) These words and phrases refer to properties of materials:
- strength ● toughness ● corrosion resistant

In the passage, there are *nine* more words which refer to properties of materials. List them below.

- _____
- _____
- _____
- _____
- _____
- _____
- _____
- _____
- _____

(b) Now write the meanings of these words. Use a dictionary if necessary.

- loosen _____
- tighten _____
- stiffen _____
- brighten _____
- cool _____

2. Nouns and adjectives

Fill in the spaces with the correct form of the word given.

Noun	Adjective
strength	strong
resistance	
	tough
hardness	

soft
brittle

'soften' means to make something softer

What words have the following meanings?
- to make something thicker _____
- to make something weaker _____
- to make something stronger _____

3. Verbs that describe change

'harden' means to make something harder

D. Check your grammar

1. ACTIVE AND PASSIVE

> **Remember**
> Hardening *is used* to make metals harder.
> A special aluminium alloy *was developed*.
> Methods of treatment *are being developed* all the time.

The sentences above are examples of passive sentences. The passive is frequently used in scientific writing because the form is impersonal and objective.

The passive is formed with 'to be', followed by the past participle of the verb: e.g. to be used, to be developed, etc.

Rewrite these sentences using the passive form instead of the active, which is underlined.

- We <u>rarely find</u> pure metals in nature.
- We <u>recover</u> metallic ores from the earth in many ways.
- We <u>obtain</u> lead from a mineral which <u>we call</u> galena.
- <u>You need</u> a lot of electrical energy to separate aluminium from the oxygen in aluminium ore.
- If <u>we add</u> lead to molten tin and then <u>cool</u> the mixture, <u>we find</u> that the freezing point of the mixture is lower than the freezing point of both lead and tin.

2. COMPARATIVES AND SUPERLATIVES

> **Remember**
> a little / a lot more than : more than : the most
> a little / a lot less than : less than : the least

Using the information in the following chart, we can say:

- The USSR produces the most iron.
- Australia produces a little more than the USA.
- Chile produces a lot less than the USSR.

Production of iron in millions of tonnes

	20	40	60	80	100	120	140
USSR							
Australia							
USA							
Canada							
Chile							

Now write five sentences about tin production using the chart below:

Production of tin in thousands of tonnes

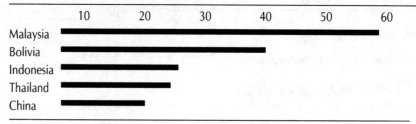

	10	20	30	40	50	60
Malaysia						
Bolivia						
Indonesia						
Thailand						
China						

3. ADVERBS AND ADJECTIVES

	Adjective		Adverb
A	careful	worker works	carefully
A	weak	metal breaks	easily
A	good	student studies	hard

Many adverbs end in '-ly' but there are exceptions, such as:
● often   ● sometimes   ● always   ● never   ● well   ● hard   ● fast
Some adverbs go with adjectives to modify them. For example:
   Aluminium is *extremely* light.
   Many alloys have been *specially* developed.

Choose either the adjective or the adverb to complete each of the sentences below:

● Alloys are general prepared by mixing molten metals.
         generally
● Pure iron is a softly metal.
         soft
● Platinum has exceptional resistance to corrosion.
         exceptionally
● Iron is easy to extract from iron ores.
      easily
● Rolled gold consists of a thin layer of gold alloy.
            thinly
● Radium is an extremely rare metal.
            rarely
● It is also highly radioactive.
      high
● Magnesium is known as a metal which burns bright.
            brightly

E. Understanding a lecture

On your tape, you will hear a lecture which contains facts referring to the different weights of metals in automobiles and to the change in amounts over a period of time. As you listen, complete the *two tables* below with the missing details:

Table 1. Typical metal content of European automobiles

Weight	Metal	Uses
	cast iron	cylinder block, gearbox
15 kg		, carburettor
		radiator pipes, electrics
	aluminium	
5 kg		battery
		vehicle body

Table 2. Typical distribution of materials in US automobiles

	1979		1985 (est.)	
	Weight, lb	%	Weight, lb	%
	2000		1500	
cast iron	515		330	13
	100	3	170	
other metals	65	2	50	2
	190	5	250	
other materials	380	12	300	10
	3250	100	2600	100

F. Understanding a printed text (2)

Read the following text carefully, looking up anything you do not understand.

DESIGN EXAMPLE—MATERIALS SYSTEMS

Engineered systems contain many components, and for each a material must be selected. The automobile is our most familiar engineering system and one that is undergoing a major change in the materials used for its construction. These trends in materials selection reflect the great effort that is being made to decrease the fuel consumption of cars by down-sizing the designs and adopting weight-saving materials. Major shifts in materials selection such as are shown in Table 6-8 can have large economic consequences.

Materials selection

Frequently, complex and severe service conditions can be met economically only by combining several materials into a single component. The surface hardening of gears and other automotive components by carburizing or nitriding[1] is a good example. Here the high hardness, strength, and wear resistance of a high-carbon steel is produced in the surface layers of a ductile and tougher low-carbon steel.

Combining materials

An excellent example of a complex materials system used in a difficult environment is the exhaust valve in an internal-combustion engine.[2] Valve materials must have excellent corrosion- and oxidation-resistance properties to resist "burning" in the temperature range 1350 to 1700°F. They must have 1) sufficient high-temperature fatigue strength and creep resistance to resist failure and 2) suitable hot hardness to resist wear and abrasion.

The critical failure regions in an exhaust valve are shown in Fig. 6-12. Maximum operating temperature occurs in areas A and C. Corrosion and oxidation resistance are especially critical there. The underhead area of the valve, area C, experiences cyclic loading, and because of the mild stress concentrations, fatigue failure may occur at that point. The valve face, area B, operates at a somewhat lower temperature because of heat conduction into the valve seat. However, if an insulating deposit builds up on the valve face, it can lead to burning. Also, the valve seat can be damaged by identation by abrasive fuel ash deposits. The valve stem is cooler than the valve head. However, wear resistance is needed. Surface wear of the valve stem, area D, can lead to scuffing, which will cause the valve to stick open and burn. Wear at the valve tip, area E, where the valve contacts the rocker arm, will cause valve lash and cause the valve to seat with higher than normal forces. Eventually, that will cause failure.

The basic valve material for passenger car application, where $T_{max} = 1300°F$, is an austenitic stainless steel that obtains its good high-temperature properties from a dispersion of precipitates. This alloy, 21-2N, contains 20.35 percent chromium for oxidation and corrosion resistance. It has good PbO corrosion resistance, and its high-temperature fatigue strength is exceeded only by that of the more expensive nickel-base super alloys, Table 6-9.

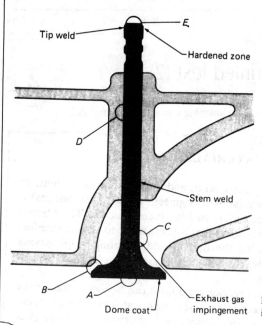

Figure 6-12 Typical exhaust valve showing critical regions of failure.

From G. Dieter *Engineering Design. A Material and Processing Approach*, pp. 192–193. McGraw-Hill.

G. Check your understanding

1. Answer the following questions:
- What is the purpose of 'down-sizing designs and adopting weight-saving materials' in the automobiles?
- What is a good example of combining several materials into a single component?
- What properties must valve materials have to resist 'burning' in extremely high temperature ranges?
- What property is necessary in the valve stem?
- What will wear at the valve tip eventually cause?

2. (a) To what, precisely, do the following refer?
- area C ● area B ● area D ● area E

(b) What can occur in the following areas, and what may be the result of it?
- area C
- area B
- area D
- area E

3. Find words in the passage which have a similar meaning and forms to those below.

- chosen
- important
- changes
- extreme

- withstand
- functions
- lead to
- touches

H. Understanding discourse

On your tape, you will hear instructions for conducting *three* simple experiments to demonstrate the effect of heat treatment on steel. Below are incomplete notes about the materials required and the steps in each experiment. As you listen, try to complete the notes. From the complete notes, write summaries of the three experiments.

Materials

two steel rods — thin and . . . ., pair of . . . .,
. . . . of sandpaper, water and . . . . source.

Experiment 1

Bend rod to measure toughness and spring. Hold rod . . . .
making sure . . . . near. Heat rod until . . . .
. . . . and dip . . . . into water.
Known as ' . . . .'. Rod has become . . . . and will
break . . . .

Experiment 2

Take . . . . rod and heat until . . . . Keep rod in
heat for about . . . . after it turns red. Remove from
heat . . . . and allow . . . . gradually.
This is 'annealing'. Rod can bend . . . .

Experiment 3

Heat . . . . rod again to bright red. Quench it and . . . .
with sandpaper. Hold it in heat again until . . . .
Rod must not become . . . . Remove rod, allow to . . . .
'Tempered' rod is . . . . but less . . . .

MEASUREMENT

A. Understanding a printed text (1)

This passage will introduce you to the principle of **measurement** in different fields of engineering. Look at the way it is divided into sections and paragraphs. Pay attention to the headings and notes in the margins, and to the table and illustration.

Now look at these questions and read the passage through to find the answers. Remember, you do not have to understand every word in order to do so.

1. Are engineering projects possible without knowledge of measurement?
2. How many types of temperature measurement are given in the third paragraph?
3. Do engineers need to know about all the different forms of measurement?
4. How many basic units is SI based on?
5. What instrument is used when measuring a flywheel housing?

Measurement

The importance of measurement

One definition. A simple dictionary definition of the verb 'to measure' is: to find the size, quantity, volume, degree, weight, etc. of something by means of a standard or unit. In all branches of engineering, measurement plays a vital role since the design, manufacture and use of any product cannot be considered without reference to this concept. 5

It is for this reason that the majority of texts on engineering contain tables, charts, lists or appendixes which provide the student with accepted standards and units of measurement.

Types of measurement

Knowledge of measurement. We are all familiar with the symbols C and F for scales of temperature, but there is also K (Kelvin), which is the fraction 10 (1/273.16) of the thermodynamic temperature of the triple part of water. Of course it may not always be necessary to understand the precise definition itself, provided one can understand the significance of the term or figure in relation to the diagram, chart or calculation involved. Each branch of engineering, naturally, tends to be more concerned with some particular 15 forms of measurement than with others.

Different systems

Conversion factors and SI equivalents. Look, for example, at Table 1 below, taken from a text for chemical engineers and which shows conversion factors. Then compare it with Table 2 which gives US customary units and their SI equivalents and comes from a text on sanitation engineering. At 20 first glance, it may seem difficult, or even impossible, to find any connection between the two. However, if we look more closely, we will see that much of the information shown deals with the same things but from a different approach. Clearly, students in either of the engineering branches for which the texts were written would have little difficulty in using the figures and 25 symbols relating to their own specialization.

Table 1

Quantity	Conversion
Length	$1(m) = 100(cm)$
	$= 3.28084(ft)$
	$= 39.3701(in)$
Mass	$1(kg) = 10^3(g)$
	$= 2.20462(lb_m)$
Force	$1(N) = 1(kg)(m)/(s)^2$
	$= 10^5(dyn)$
	$= 0.224809(lb_f)$
Pressure	$1(bar) = 10^5(kg)/(m)(s)^2$
	$= 10^5(N)/(m)^2$
	$= 10^6(dyn)/(cm)^2$
	$= 0.986923(atm)$
	$= 14.5038(psia)$
	$= 750.061(mm\ Hg)$
Volume	$1(m)^3 = 10^6(cm)^3$
	$= 10^3(l)$
	$= 35.3147(ft)^3$
	$= 264.172(gal)$
Density	$1(g)/(cm)^3 = 10^3(kg)/(m)^3$
	$= 10^3(g)/(l)$
	$= 62.4278(lb_m)/(ft)^3$
	$= 8.34540(lb_m)/(gal)$
Energy	$1(J) = 1(kg)(m)^2/(s)^2$
	$= 1(N \cdot m)$
	$= 1(W \cdot s)$
	$= 10^7(dyn \cdot cm)$
	$= 10^7(erg)$
	$= 10(cm)^3(bar)$
	$= 10^{-2}(l \cdot bar)$
	$= 10^{-5}(m)^3(bar)$
	$= 0.239006(cal)$
	$= 9.86923(cm)^3(atm)$
	$= 5.12197 \times 10^{-3}(ft)^3(psia)$
	$= 0.737562(ft \cdot lb_f)$
	$= 9.47831 \times 10^{-4}(Btu)$
Power	$1(kW) = 10^3(kg)(m)^2/(s)^3$
	$= 10^3(W)$
	$= 10^3(J)/(s)$
	$= 10^3(V \cdot A)$
	$= 239.006(cal)/(s)$
	$= 737.562(ft \cdot lb_f)/(s)$
	$= 56.8699(Btu)/(min)$
	$= 1.34102(HP)$

(Smith & Van Ness, *Introduction to Chemical Engineering Thermodynamics*, McGraw-Hill, 1975.)

Table 2

Quantity	U.S. customary unit	SI equivalent
Area	mi^2	$2.590\ km^2$
	acre	$4047\ m^2$
	ft^2	$0.0929\ m^2$
	in^2	$645.2\ mm^2$
Concentration	lb/million gal	0.1200 mg/l
Energy	$ft \cdot lb$	1.356 J
Force	lb	4.448 N
Flow	ft^3/s	$0.0283\ m^3/s$
	gal/min	$0.003785\ m^3/min$
Length	ft	0.3048 m
	in	25.40 mm
	mi	1.609 km
Mass	grain	64.80 mg
	oz	28.35 g
	lb	0.4536 kg
	ton	907.2 kg
Power	$ft \cdot lb/s$	1.356 W
	hp	745.7 W
Pressure	lb/ft^2	47.88 Pa
	lb/in^2	6.895 kPa
	ft (of water)	2.988 kPa
Velocity	ft/s	0.3048 m/s
	in/s	0.0254 m/s
	gal/ft^2 per min	0.0407 m/min
		58.678 m/day
	gal/ft^2 per day	0.0407 m/day
	ft^3	$0.02832\ m^3$
	yd^3	$0.7646\ m^3$
Volume	gal	$0.003785\ m^3$
	$acre \cdot ft$	$1233.5\ m^3$

(Steel & McGhee, *Water Supply and Sewerage*. McGraw-Hill, 1979.)

SI Units. SI is the abbreviation for *Système International d'Unités*. SI is based on seven basic units, each of which is defined with great accuracy and from which all other basic units are derived. Under the system, each physical quantity has only one particular unit for its measurement. Thus, a **30** length is only measured in metres. If the number employed with a basic unit is very small, or very large, then a prefix can be used as in km for kilometres.

The basis of SI

Conversion tables are necessary because the USA and Britain still retain a measurement system which is different from that used by the rest of the world.

Measuring devices. Since measurement is so important, it follows that there **35** is a wide range of devices and instruments which are designed to indicate very precisely length, pressure, time and so on. The illustration below, from a manual on diesel mechanics, with its instructions for aligning and measuring a flywheel housing, shows one such device and some of the **40** language and figures associated with its use.

Aligning and Measuring Flywheel Housing

When you install a new flywheel housing, you must position it to permit the axis of the crankshaft to be concentric with the flywheel-housing bore. To check the position of the flywheel housing, screw an indicator holder or place a magnetic base onto the crankshaft. Attach a dial gauge to it so that the pointer rests squarely on the surface of the bore (Fig. 16-3). Zero the dial, then turn the crankshaft one complete revolution. Record readings at 90° intervals. The reading at any point must not exceed an average concentricity (runout) tolerance of 0.005 in [0.12 mm]. Tap the housing into alignment and tighten the hex bolts.

Your next check should be the flywheel-housing face runout. To make this check, relocate the dial gauge so that the pointer rests against the flywheel-housing flange. Force the crankshaft forward to remove end play, then zero the dial. Turn the crankshaft one complete revolution, and record readings at 90° intervals. *(NOTE: Make sure the crankshaft is placed forward when taking the readings.)* The average allowable maximum face runout is about 0.010 in [0.25 mm].

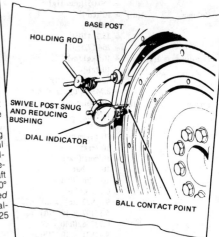

Labels: BASE POST · HOLDING ROD · SWIVEL POST SNUG AND REDUCING BUSHING · DIAL INDICATOR · BALL CONTACT POINT

E.J. Schulz, *Diesel Mechanics*, p 91. McGraw-Hill, 1985.

B. Check your understanding

1. Read the text again carefully, looking up anything you do not understand in a dictionary
or reference book. Then answer the following questions:

1. What is measurement?

2. How many different symbols for measurement of length are shown in the two tables?

3. How is the US measurement of force different from the SI unit?

4. Why do you think flow, concentration and velocity are in Table 2 but not in Table 1?

5. What is the principle on which SI is based?

6. What is the US customary unit for the SI equivalent 1.356J?

7. How many 'ins' are there in 1 'm', according to Table 1?

8. In the instructions on flywheel alignment, does 90° refer to temperature or distance?

2. Look at the text and say what the following words refer to:

- line   5: concept
- line   6: reason
- line 13: one
- line 19: it
- line 24: branches
- line 28: which
- line 34: that
- line 41: its

3. Look at Table (a) and Conversion Chart (b). Are the facts shown below true (T) or false (F)?

Table (a)

- $1J = 0.239006$ cal ☐
- $1m^3 = 35.3147(ft)^2$ ☐
- $10^3(W) = 1kW$ ☐
- 14.503 (psia) $= 2$ bar ☐

Chart (b)

- $1in = 25.40$ cm ☐
- 907.2 kg $= 1$ ton ☐
- $1 lb/in^2 = 6.895kPa$ ☐
- 1 acre $= 4047m^3$ ☐

C. Increase your vocabulary

1. Find the symbols in Tables 1 and 2 which match the words:

- Joule
- inch
- mile
- Watt
- horse power
- kilogram
- miles per second
- pounds per square foot
- cubic metre
- milligrams per litre

2. Now look at the first paragraph, and say:
- What words could you replace with 'using'?
- What word has the same meaning as 'very important'?
- What does 'accepted' mean here?

3. Fill in the following table:

Noun	Verb
design	
product	
significance	
calculation	
connection	
information	
specialisation	
instructions	

4. The word 'zero' in *Aligning and measuring flywheel housing* can be a verb or a noun with the same spelling. Find 10 more verbs in the section which can also be nouns like this:

Noun	Verb
a screw	to screw

▼

D. Check your grammar

1.

Rewrite the following sentences using can / should / must / may with the passive form.

- Next, you should check the flywheel-housing face runout.
- You must position the flywheel housing very precisely.
- You can check the position by placing a magnetic base onto the crankshaft.
- It is possible to convert miles into kilometres by multiplying by 1.609.
- You can express the multiple 10^6 using the prefix mega and you must use M as the symbol for this.
- With SI numbers, you should not use a comma to separate multiples of a thousand. You may use a space instead.

2.

Complete the following sentences with — like / unlike / whereas / although / however — so that they make sense.

- _____ the SI unit for force is the newton (N), the US customary unit is the pound (lb).
- One acre seems to be very different from 4047m^2 at first glance. _____, both figures denote the same area.
- Daily temperature in Europe is expressed in Celsius (°C), _____ in the USA where Fahrenheit (°F) is used.
- A diesel engine requires no ignition system _____ a gasoline engine cannot operate without one.
- _____ the gasoline engine, the diesel engine is of the internal combustion design since they both burn fuel within the cylinders.

3. *DEFINING*

Make similar statements to the three above using the information in this table.

Term	Class	Function
Barometer		measure strength of electric current
Compass	device	measure altitude of the sun
Ammeter		calculate rapidly
Slide rule	instrument	measure atmospheric pressure
Micrometer	tool	measure very small distances
Sextant		determine direction

E. Understanding a lecture

On your tape, you will hear part of a lecture. It has been divided into sections to enable you to understand it more easily. After each section, answer the following questions.

Section 1

1. Is this the first lecture the speaker has given to the class? If not, how do you know?
2. What is the subject of this lecture?
3. Does the lecturer specify an exact number of ways to classify measuring devices?

Section 2

1. Complete the classification diagram below with the three categories mentioned by the lecturer.
2. What examples are given for category b?
3. Are other types of classification possible?

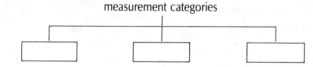

measurement categories

Section 3

1. Complete the top section of the classification diagram below.
2. Give an example of each of the units shown in the top section of the diagram.

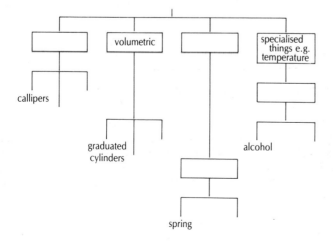

volumetric

specialised things e.g. temperature

callipers

graduated cylinders

alcohol

spring

1. Complete as much of the rest of the diagram as possible with the examples of measuring devices mentioned in this section of the lecture.
2. Where are measuring cups and measuring spoons usually found?

1. Complete the diagram now with the relevant information on specialised measuring devices.
2. How does the household thermometer function, according to the lecturer?

Summarising After checking that your classification diagrams are correct by listening to the tape, be prepared to use either of them to give a short talk on measuring devices and how they can be classified. You should refer to the diagrams as you talk. Then choose one measuring device and write a brief explanation about the way it can be classified.

F. Understanding a printed text (2)

Read the following passage, looking up anything you do not understand.

Consumption of Water

1.

Population density, considering a whole city, rarely exceeds an average of 7500 to 10,000 per km² (30 to 40 per acre). More important to the engineer, in solving water and sewerage problems, are the densities in particular areas, since he must design sewers and water mains so that each section of the city will be adequately served. Densities vary widely within a city, the general range being from 3800 per 5 km² (15 per acre) in the sparsely built-up residential sections to 8800 to 10,000 per km² (35 to 40 per acre) in closely built-up single-family residential areas with small lots. In apartment and tenement districts the populations will be 25,000 to 250,000 per km² (100 to 1000 per acre). In commercial districts the day population 10 will be highly variable according to development.

2.

The water furnished to a city can be classified according to its ultimate use or end. The uses are:

(a)   This includes water furnished to houses, hotels, etc., for sanitary, culin-
ary, drinking, washing, bathing, and other purposes. It varies according to
living conditions of consumers, the range usually being considered as 75 to **15**
380 l (20 to 100 gal) per capita per day, averaging 190 to 340 l (50 to 90 gal)
per capita. These figures include air conditioning of residences and irrigation

or sprinkling of privately owned gardens and lawns, a practice that may have a considerable effect upon total consumption in some parts of the country. The domestic consumption may be expected to be about 50 percent of the total in the average city; but where the total consumption is small, the proportion will be much greater. 20

(b) Water so classified is that furnished to industrial and commercial plants. Its importance will depend upon local conditions, such as the existence of large industries, and whether or not the industries patronize 25 the public waterworks. Self-supplied industrial water requirements are estimated to be more than 200 percent of municipal water supply demand.

The quantity of water required for commercial and industrial use has been related to the floor area of buildings served. Symons proposes an average of 12.2 m^3/1000 m^2 of floor area per day (0.3 gal/ft^2 per day). In cities of 30 over 25,000 population commercial consumption may be expected to amount to about 15 percent of the total consumption.

(c) Public buildings, such as city halls, jails, and schools, as well as public service—flushing streets and fire protection—require much water for which, usually, the city is not paid. Such water amounts to 50 to 75 l per capita. The 35 actual amount of water used for extinguishing fires does not figure greatly in the average consumption, but very large fires will cause the rate of use to be high for short periods.

(d) This water is sometimes classified as "unaccounted for," although some of the loss and waste may be accounted for in the sense that its cause 40 and amount are approximately known. Unaccounted-for water is due to meter and pump slippage, unauthorized water connections and leaks in mains. It is apparent that the unaccounted-for water, and also waste by customers, can be reduced by careful maintenance of the water system and by universal metering of all water services. In a system 100 percent metered and 45 moderately well maintained, the unaccounted-for water, exclusive of pump slippage, will be about 10 percent.

Table 2-1 Projected consumption of water for various purposes in the year 2000[1]

Use	Liters per capita/day†	Percentage of total
Domestic	300	44
Industrial	160	24
Commercial	100	15
Public	60	9
Loss and waste	50	8
Total	670	100

† Gallons = liters × 0.264

The total consumption will be the sum of the foregoing uses and the loss and waste. The probable division of this consumption is shown in Table 2-1. Table 2-2 shows some total consumptions as reported in cities in various parts of the **50** country. The average daily per capita consumption may be taken to be 670 l (175 gal). This means little, however, as individual figures vary widely. Each city has to be studied, particularly with regard to industrial and commercial uses and actual or probable loss and waste. Care must also be taken in considering per capita figures since the figure may be based upon persons actually served or upon **55** census population of the city.

Table 2-2 Recorded rates of water consumption in some American cities

City	Average daily per capita consumption, l†	Maximum one-day consumption in a 3-year period, l	Maximum in proportion to average, %
Rochester, N.Y.	451	637	141
Syracuse, N.Y.	728	917	126
Hartford, Conn.	671	887	132
Albany, N.Y.	671	860	128
El Paso, Tex.	447	739	165
Portland, Me.	572	773	135
Camden, N.J.	641	963	150
Albuquerque, N.M.	402	766	190
Winston-Salem, N.C.	447	580	130
Waterloo, Iowa	383	625	163
Passaic, N.J.	807	1016	126

Steel & McGhee, *Water Supply and Sewerage*, pp 12–19. McGraw-Hill, 1979.

G. Check your understanding

1. Indicate the proper location in the reading passage of the headings and sub-headings below by placing the appropriate number or letter after them.

- Consumption for Various Purposes
- Commercial and Industrial
- Domestic
- Density of Population
- Loss and Waste
- Public Use

2. Are the statements below correct or incorrect according to the information given in the passage?

- Population density over the whole city is the most important factor for an engineer in solving water and sewerage problems. ☐

- The day population in commercial districts is difficult to calculate accurately. ☐

- Water for washing, drinking, cooking, etc. usually amounts to about half of the daily total used in cities. ☐
- Industrial and commercial plants do not always use the public water system. ☐
- The amount of commercial water consumption is related to the size of the population in a city. ☐
- Cities do not receive payment for water used to fight fires or in public buildings. ☐
- It is not known how much water is lost or wasted in cities. ☐
- Every person in America uses 670 litres of water per day. ☐
- Albuquerque had the lowest average daily per capita consumption, according to Table 2–2: ☐

- The highest recorded maximum in proportion to average consumption in percentage terms belongs to El Paso. ☐

3. Find words in the passage which have similar forms and meanings to those below:

- is higher than
- changeable
- made available to
- homes
- make use of
- is equal to
- illegal
- not including

4. To what do the following figures refer?

- 8800 to 10 000 per km^2
- 100 litres per capita/day
- $12.2m^3/1000m^2$
- 50 to 75 l per capita
- 141 %

H. Understanding discourse

Listen to your tape. You will hear two students talking. One student has a problem and the other is helping him. They are practising the correct way to write and say the numbers and equations which are in the charts and conversion tables. Listen to the tape twice. As you listen for the second time, try to answer the questions below.

1. Write down the three numbers or equations the students practise.
1.
2.
3.

2. The second student uses two phrases to make a suggestion. Complete the suggestions below with the words he uses.
1. _____ say some and you can write them down now?
2. _____ check.

3. The second student uses one of the phrases again. Write down what he says.
1.
2.

4. 1. What two symbols can be used to express decimals?
2. Write down the words which express the following:
- $10 \ cm^3$
- $5 \ in^2$
- $101 \ m^3$

5. The second student gives advice to the first student. Complete the statements below with the words he uses.
1. _____ to say oh and not zero in decimals.
2. _____ say cubic metres per minute.

6. Work with a partner. Choose a number or an equation from the charts in your book. He writes down what you say. Then you write down what he says. Practise three numbers or equations each.

A. Understanding a printed text (1)

This text gives you some information about the design and function of **filters** in diesel systems. Remember to look at the notes in the margins for quick reference and notice how the text is divided into paragraphs of different lengths. Pay attention to the diagrams and labels.

Try to answer the following questions after the first reading. Remember, you do not have to understand every word in the text to do so.

1. What is the function of a filter?
2. How many classes of filter materials are mentioned?
3. Which materials are only used for the exhaust system?
4. How many basic types of filter are used?
5. Which type of filter is used mainly for the lubrication and fuel injection systems?

Filters for diesel systems

The need for filters in systems

1 The most common cause of engine trouble is contaminants in the system; therefore, the most sensible way to maintain and preserve a high-performance hydraulic system is simply to keep the system clean. Many different types of filters are manufactured to accommodate the various types of hydraulic systems. Filters are a lifeline because they remove contaminants and thus protect the system. The manufacturers originally install the filters, strainers, and breathers. They also provide service manuals with precise instructions in order to ensure troublefree operation of the system components. Nevertheless, foreign matter enters the system usually through careless or inadequate maintenance, or through normal wear of the components within the system.

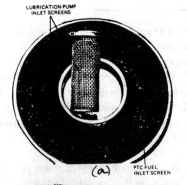

LUBRICATION-PUMP
INLET SCREENS

(a) PTC FUEL
INLET SCREEN

2 There are three classes of filter materials: mechanical, inactive absorbent, and active absorbent. The mechanical filter consists of closely woven metal screens or metal disks. It generally removes only fairly coarse insoluble particles.

Materials used in filter elements

3 Inactive absorbent filters are composed of materials such as cotton, yarn, cloth, impregnated cellulose paper, or porous metal. They will remove quite small particles and some types even remove water and water-soluble contaminants. The elements often are treated to give them an affinity to the contaminants found in the system.

(b)

4 Active absorbent filter materials, such as charcoal or Fuller's earth, remove particles by absorption as well as by filtering. They are *not* used as filter material for the lubrication or fuel-injection systems. They are, however, used as a filter material for the exhaust system.

Measurement of filter effectiveness

5 The unit of measurement for determining the effectiveness of a filter is the *micrometer* (μm) (old term: micron). One micrometer is equal to 0.000039 inch (1 μm = 0.000039 in), or in metric units of measurement, 0.000001 meter (1 μm = 0.000001 m). When new and clean, a filter will prevent a specific percentage of particles measuring a specific minimum size from entering the fluid.

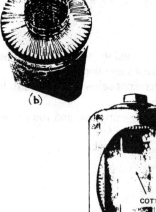

COTTON

(c)

6　　　　　Four basic types of filters are used: screen and strainer, surface type, deep type, and edge type. The type, size, and micrometer rating is dictated by the system itself.

7 SCREENS AND STRAINERS　Screens or strainers are surface-type filters and sometimes are referred to as mechanical filters (Fig. 22-1). These inlet screens prevent large foreign particles from entering the system. They are classified according to a sieve number which relates to the micrometer rating.

8 SURFACE-TYPE FILTER　The surface-type filter element shown in Fig. 22-2a is composed of a specially treated micrometric cellulose paper. The paper is formed in vertical convolutions (wrinkles) and in a cylindrical pattern. It is reinforced on the inside and outside and is equipped with a seal on the top and bottom. Sometimes multifolded paper elements are used.

9 DEEP-TYPE FILTER　The design of the deep-type filter is quite different from that of the surface filter (see Fig. 22-2b). It is more efficient and has a longer service life. Figure 22-3 shows two types of filter materials and illustrates the substantial depth of the filter material.

10　Deep-type filters of porous materials consist of fine woven copper or cinder bronze elements formed to fit the filter housing (Fig. 22-4). They can also be made of minute stainless steel balls joined as one inflexible piece.

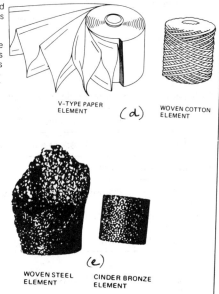

V-TYPE PAPER ELEMENT　(d)　WOVEN COTTON ELEMENT

WOVEN STEEL ELEMENT　(e)　CINDER BRONZE ELEMENT

Different types of filters

11 EDGE-TYPE FILTER　Edge-type filters are used as primary filters for the lubrication and fuel-injection systems. In this design, many copper, bronze, paper, or steel disks are positioned over the center tube. The tube acts as a hydraulic line and directs oil to the outlet port. Some edge-type filters have the added convenience of an automatic scraper or a hand-operated scraper for cleaning the outside of the disk (Fig. 22-5). This, of course, helps to extend the life of the filter.

12　　　　　Regardless of the design or the type of a filter element, a filter element is sealed in a housing. O rings or gaskets separate the filtered from the unfiltered liquid. Liquid enters near the top of the filter housing or, with a screw-on-type oil or fuel filter, it enters via the adapter plate, and flows into the outer area of the filter element (Fig. 22-6). The system pressure forces the liquid through the filter element into the center area. Filtered liquid then passes through the center and on to the outlet port. Some filter designs incorporate an antidrain check valve to prevent fluid from draining from the filter bowl when the engine is stopped. This ensures instant oil or fuel pressure when restarting.

13　Full-flow oil filters have either a built-in bypass valve or a bypass valve which is mounted separately. The purpose of the bypass valve is to bypass oil ensuring lubricant to the system in the event that the filter element becomes plugged. A bypass valve is also used in oil coolers for the same purpose.

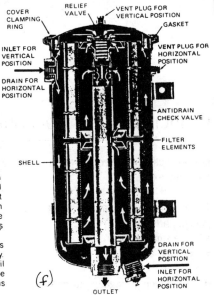

COVER CLAMPING RING
RELIEF VALVE
VENT PLUG FOR VERTICAL POSITION
GASKET
INLET FOR VERTICAL POSITION
VENT PLUG FOR HORIZONTAL POSITION
DRAIN FOR HORIZONTAL POSITION
ANTIDRAIN CHECK VALVE
FILTER ELEMENTS
SHELL
DRAIN FOR VERTICAL POSITION
INLET FOR HORIZONTAL POSITION
(f)
OUTLET

How liquid flows through a filter

E.J. Schulz, *Diesel Mechanics*, pp 151–152. McGraw-Hill, 1985.

B. Check your understanding

Read the text again carefully, looking up anything you do not understand in a dictionary or reference book. Then do the following exercises.

1. By reference to the text, answer these questions.

1. What Figure references should the letters below the illustrations indicate?

2. Which type of filter is not illustrated here?

3. What exactly does Fig. 22–6 illustrate?

4. What are two causes of contaminants in a system?

5. Can filters prevent all particles from entering a system?

6. What is the connection between Screens and Strainers and Surface-Type filters?

7. Which type of filter can use metal or paper elements?

8. What feature is common to all filter elements?

2. What do the following words refer to?

- paragraph 1, line 10: they
- paragraph 2, line 5: it
- paragraph 4, line 4: they
- paragraph 8, line 5: it
- paragraph 11, line 3: this
- paragraph 12, line 13: this

3. Are the sentences below True (T) or False (F) according to the information given in the text?

- Engine trouble is often caused by contaminants in the system. ☐
- All inactive absorbent filters can remove water. ☐
- Charcoal is a material used in active absorbent filters. ☐
- A micron and a micrometer indicate the same unit of measurement. ☐
- Mechanical filters are different from surface-type filters. ☐
- Disks in edge-type filters are made of paper. ☐

C. Increase your vocabulary

Using a dictionary if necessary, complete the following exercises.

1. Say what words are used in the first paragraph to mean:
- to be suitable for
- accurate and detailed steps in maintenance
- parts which go together to make up a system

2. In paragraphs 2, 3 and 4, find two verbs which can mean 'to be made up of'

3. Explain in your own words the meaning of the following phrases, which occur in the first four paragraphs:
- a high-performance hydraulic system
- water-soluble contaminants
- fuel-injection systems

4. Say which words in paragraphs 6–11 have the opposite meanings to the following:
- allow
- horizontal
- inefficient
- non-porous
- very large
- reduce

5. Find the prepositions which usually follow these verbs.
- to be composed . . .
- to consist . . .
- to classify according . . .
- to be made . . .
- to act . . .
- to relate . . .
- to be different . . .
- to be equipped . . .

6. Some of the texts in this book are written in American English, in which certain words are spelt differently from the usual form in British English. One example is *center* (American)/*centre* (British). Have you noticed any others?

Start a list in your notebook and keep it up to date as you work through this book.

D. Check your grammar

1. *PREPOSITIONS DENOTING LOCATION AND MOVEMENT*

> **Remember**
> - The tube directs oil *to* the outlet port.
> - Liquid enters *near* the top of the filter housing.

Use the following words to complete the passage below; you may use some of the words more than once:
- in ● via ● into ● through ● to.

Liquid Flow _____ Filters

Regardless of the design or the type of the filter element, a filter element is sealed _____ a housing. Liquid enters near the top of the filter housing or _____ the adaptor plate. Then, it flows _____ the outer area of the filter element. The system pressure forces the liquid _____ the filter element _____ the centre area. Filtered liquid then passes _____ the centre and on _____ the outlet port. Some filter designs have an antidrain check valve to prevent fluid from draining _____ the filter bowl when the engine is stopped. This ensures instant oil or fuel pressure when restarting.

2. *INDEFINITE AND DEFINITE ARTICLES*

> **Remember:**
> - Filters are *a* lifeline because they remove contaminants and protect *the* system.
> - *A* bypass valve is also used in oil coolers for *the* same purpose.
> - Some edge-type filters have *an* automatic scraper to clean the outside of the *disk*.

Supply or omit as required 'a', 'an' or 'the' in these sentences. Note that a line does not always mean that a word is necessary:

1. ___ unit of ___ measurement for determining ___ effectiveness of ___ filter is ___ micrometer.
2. After ___ iron has been made in ___ blast-furnace, it contains ___ lot of ___ carbon. This means that ___ iron is brittle. ___ steel is stronger and less brittle than ___ iron it is made of.
3. ___ special paper in ___ surface-type filter element is reinforced on ___ inside and outside and is equipped with ___ seal on ___ top and bottom.
4. ___ surface-type filters are classified according to ___ sieve number which relates to ___ micrometer rating.
5. ___ design of ___ deep-type filter is quite different from that of ___ surface filter. It is also more efficient and has ___ longer service life.

▼

The examples below show how some verbs are used to describe how something is made ('design') and some verbs describe how something works ('function'):

> *Design:*
> Some filter types *incorporate* an antidrain check valve.
> *Function:*
> A filter *prevents* particles *from entering* the fluid.

(a) Use D (design) or F (function) after these verbs to show what they express. For example: to incorporate — Ⓓ

- to be composed of ☐
- to separate ☐
- to maintain ☐
- to consist of ☐
- to be formed from ☐

- to be used as ☐
- to remove ☐
- to ensure ☐
- to be made of ☐
- to act as ☐

(b) Now select the right verbs from the above list and use them in the correct form to write complete sentences based on the prompts given below:

- Edge-type filters _____ primary filters for the lubrication system.
- The mechanical filter _____ closely woven metal screens or disks.
- Inactive absorbent filters _____ quite small particles.
- Antidrain check valves in filters _____ instant oil or fuel pressure when restarting.
- Deep-type filters can _____ minute stainless steel balls joined as one inflexible piece.

E. Understanding a lecture

On your tape, you will hear part of a lecture. Answer the questions and complete the diagrams below according to the information you hear:

. . . . and Mathematical Modelling

Section 1——————————————————————————

1. What has the lecture been about up to this point?
2. Supply the missing words in the title above.

Section 2——————————————————————————

1. How are the four illustrations related?
2. Why do the students have to supply the missing details?

Section 3——————————————————————————

1. What system is shown by the four diagrams?
2. How does the lecturer refer to the elements of the system?
3. What can be used to describe the behaviour of the idealised elements of the system?

Section 4————————————————————————————————

Supply the missing words in the diagram below:

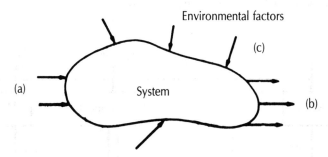

1. Characteristics of the Modelling Process.

Section 5————————————————————————————————

Supply the missing words in the diagram below:

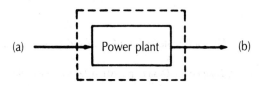

2. Overall Model for a Steam Power Plant.

Section 6————————————————————————————————

Supply the missing words in the diagram below:

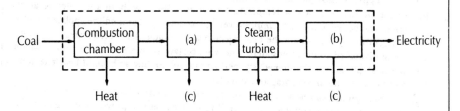

3. Block Diagram of Major Components of Power Plant.

Section 7————————————————————————————————

1. Name three obvious factors an engineer must consider in relation to some of the
   components shown in Diagram 3.
2. Name one finer detail important in the design process.

1. Label the pumps on the diagram below.
2. Write in the word 'water' to show its flow.
3. Supply the other missing words in the diagram.
4. What is of great importance concerning waste gases?

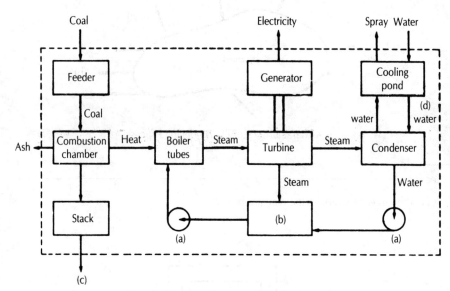

4. Detailed Systems for a Coal-Fired Power Plant.

Diagrams from: G. Dieter, *Engineering Design*, pp 101–102. McGraw-Hill, 1983.

F. Understanding a printed text (2)

Read the following text carefully, looking up anything you do not understand.

Heat Pumps

Application and classification of heat pumps

1   **Types of heat pumps** All refrigeration systems are heat pumps, because they absorb heat energy at a low temperature level and discharge it to a high temperature level. The designation *heat pump*, however, has developed around the application of a refrigeration system where the heat rejected at the condenser is used instead of simply being dissipated to the atmosphere. There are certain applications and occasions where the heat pump can simultaneously perform useful cooling and useful heat rejection, and this is clearly an advantageous situation.

2   Heat pumps can be and often are applied in a variety of contexts. Four important classifications this chapter explores are (1) package heat pumps with a reversible cycle, (2) decentralized heat pumps for air-conditioning moderate- and large-sized buildings, (3) heat pumps with a double-bundle condenser, and (4) industrial heat pumps. Common threads run through all four categories, but each group also responds to a unique opportunity or need.

3   **Package type, reversible cycle** This classification especially includes residential and small commercial units that are capable of heating a space in cold weather and cooling it in warm weather. The several different sources and sinks from which the heat pump can draw its heat or reject it—air, water, earth—will be discussed For purposes of explanation air will be initially assumed to be the source.

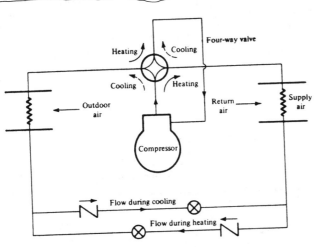

Figure 18-1 Reversible cycle air-source heat pump.

4   The reversible heat pump operates with the flow diagram shown in Fig. 18-1. During the heating operation the four-way valve positions itself so that the high-pressure discharge gas from the compressor flows first to the heat exchanger in the conditioned airstream. In its condensing process the refrigerant rejects heat, warming the air. Liquid refrigerant flows on to the expansion-device section, where the check valve in the upper line prevents flow through its branch and instead the liquid refrigerant flows through the expansion device in the lower branch. The cold low-pressure refrigerant then extracts heat from the outdoor air while it vaporizes. Refrigerant vapor returns to the four-way valve to be directed to the suction side of the compressor.

Operation of the reversible heat pump

5   To convert from heating to cooling operation the four-way valve shifts to its opposite position so that discharge gas from the compressor first flows to the outdoor coil, where the refrigerant rejects heat during condensation. After passing through the expansion device in the upper branch of Fig. 18-1, the low-pressure low-temperature refrigerant evaporates in the heat exchanger that cools air from the conditioned space.

6   Two branches for the expansion device are needed in Fig. 18-1, because a conventional superheat-controlled expansion valve would perform properly with flow only in one direction. It might seem that a capillary tube would work satisfactorily, because its performance is the same regardless of direction of flow, but the pressure difference across the capillary tube is much higher during winter heating operation than during summer cooling. Thus a capillary tube sized for one season is improperly sized for the other. The electric expansion valve can operate with refrigerant flow in either direction.

Expansion devices

▼

7   **Decentralized heat pump** A feature of the decentralized-heat-pump arrangement, as shown schematically in Fig. 18-7, is that it can pump heat from zones of a building that require cooling to other zones that require heating. The heat pumps in this concept are water-to-air units, each serving its own zone. A water loop serves these heat pumps, which automatically switch between heating and cooling as needed to maintain the desired space temperature. If most of the heat pumps are in the cooling mode, the temperature of the loop water rises and when t_{ret} reaches about 32°C, three-way valve I diverts water flow to the heat rejector. This heat rejector discharges heat to the atmosphere through the use of an air-cooled finned coil or an evaporative cooler. If most of the heat pumps are in the heating mode, t_{ret} drops and three-way valve I sends the water straight through; and if t_{ret} drops to 15°C, three-way valve II opens to the fuel-fired or electric heater to make up the heating deficiency of the system.

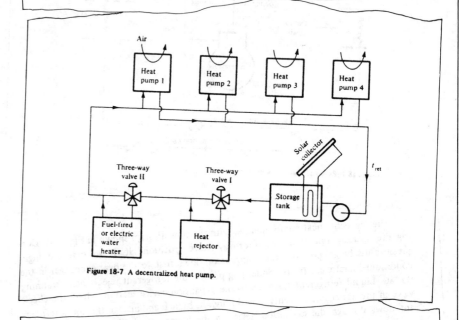

Figure 18-7 A decentralized heat pump.

8   The heat rejector and supplementary heater are necessary components of all decentralized-heat-pump systems, but the storage tank and solar collector are options. The storage tank is effective on days when net heat is rejected from the building during the day (because of solar load, lights, warm outdoor temperatures, etc.), and the system has a heat deficiency at night. The water in the storage tank rises in temperature during the day and provides a source of heat for nighttime operation. The incorporation of the solar collector converts the system into a solar-assisted heat pump.

9   **Double-bundle condenser** During cold weather large buildings may require heat at the perimeter zones although the interior zones are unaffected by the outdoor conditions and always require cooling. One type of internal-source heat pump that pumps heat from the interior zones to the perimeter zones is the heat pump with a double-bundle condenser. One arrangement of this system is shown in Fig. 18-9, where a cooling tower cools water for one of the bundles and the water for the heating coils in the perimeter zones flows through the other bundle.

10   The strategy of operation is that the compressor (usually of the centrifugal type in these systems) have its capacity regulated to maintain t_1 at a constant value, say, 6°C. The controller of the hot-water-supply temperature modulates valve V1 to divert more water to the cooling tower if t_2 rises too high. As t_2 begins to drop, V1 first closes off the water flow to the cooling tower. Upon a continued drop in t_2 electric heaters in the hot-water line are brought into service.

11   The cooling coil serves an air system (variable-air volume, for example) which may supply both the interior and perimeter zones. The supply-air temperature t_3 could be held constant at 13°C by modulating valve V2. The net result of the operation is that heat removed from the air being cooled is supplied to heating needs. When excess heat is available, it is rejected through the cooling tower. A deficiency of heat for the heating coils is compensated for through the use of electric heaters.

Operation of the double-bundle condenser heat pump

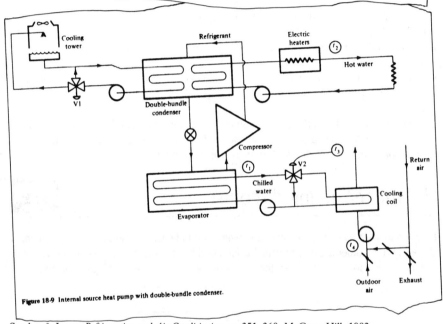

Figure 18-9 Internal source heat pump with double-bundle condenser.

Stoeker & Jones, *Refrigeration and Air Conditioning*, pp 351–360. McGraw-Hill, 1982.

G. Check your understanding

1. Answer the following questions on the text. You may use a dictionary if necessary:

1. What is the basic application of a heat pump?
2. Which classification of heat pump does the text omit?
3. What two opposite functions does the reversible cycle heat pump perform?
4. What is the function of the check valve in the upper line of Figure 18–1?
5. How does the four-way valve convert from heating to cooling?
6. Why is a capillary tube not suitable in this type of pump?
7. What is the main feature of the decentralised heat pump?
8. How do these heat pumps switch between heating and cooling?
9. At what temperature does the three-way valve I divert water flow?
10. What are not necessary components of these systems?
11. Describe one function of the heat pump with double-bundle condensers.
12. What device has its capacity regulated to maintain temperature at 6°C?
13. What happens if t_2 continues to drop?
14. What is rejected through the cooling tower?

2. Find words in the text which can replace these expressions:
- at the same time
- does not accept
- to change
- changes to vapour
- without manual control
- additional
- a shortage of heat
- kept unchanged

3. Find the words in the text which express these phrases in a simpler form:

- gas which is pushed out under high pressure
- a valve which operates in four different ways
- refrigerant which is stored under low pressure and at a low temperature
- units which transfer heat from water into the atmosphere

4. Can you explain these sentences in your own words?

- For purposes of explanation air will be initially assumed to be the source [end paragraph 3].
- Thus a capillary tube sized for one season is improperly sized for the other [end paragraph 6].
- A deficiency of heat for the heating coils is compensated for through the use of electric heaters [end paragraph 11].

5. Now read the section on the decentralised heat pump again and be prepared to give orally or to write an explanation — in your own words, where possible — about the way this type of pump provides heat to areas which require it.

H. Understanding discourse

1. Listen to your tape. You will hear a conversation between two students. One of them is new and the other is explaining the location of different buildings on the university site to him. As you listen, write down the names of the buildings on the diagram below.

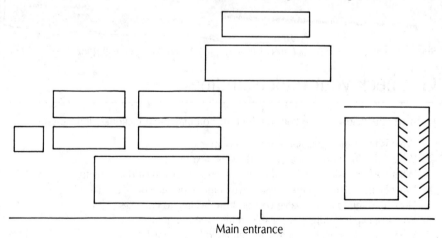

Main entrance

2. Now answer these questions:

1. What is the name of the new student?
2. What, besides a Student Union card, do students get in the administration building?
3. What sports does the new student play?
4. On what side of the dining room do cars leave the car park?
5. How many people work in the First Aid department?

ENERGY, HEAT AND WORK

A. Understanding a printed text (1)

The following text will give you some information about **types and sources of energy**. It will also explain briefly how energy may be converted to **work**. Note the paragraph organisation and refer to the headings in the margin for quick reference.

Now look at these questions:

1. What is the type of energy created by movement?

2. What type of energy depends upon position?
3. What type of energy comes from the sun?
4. What are the three most important sources of power?
5. Give an example of a heat engine.

Read the passage and find the answers to these questions. It is not necessary to understand every word to do this.

Energy, Heat and Work

1 Energy may be thought of as that property of something which enables it to do work. When we say that something possesses energy, we suggest that it is capable in some way of exerting a force on something else and performing work on it. When work is done on something, on the other hand, energy has been added to it. Energy is measured in the same units as those of work, the foot-pound and the joule.

What is energy?

2 Energy occurs in several forms. A familiar example is the energy a moving body possesses by virtue of its motion. Every moving object has the capacity to do work. By striking another object that is free to move, the moving object can exert a force and cause the second object to shift its position. It is not necessary that the moving object actually do work; it may keep on moving, or friction may slowly bring it to a stop. But while it is moving, it has the *capacity* for doing work. It is this specific property that defines energy, since energy means the ability to do work, and so all moving things have energy by virtue of their motion. This type of energy is called *kinetic energy*.

Kinetic energy

3 The statement that energy is the capacity something has to do work is not restricted to kinetic energy but is perfectly general. Many objects possess energy because of their *position*. Consider a pile driver, a simple machine that lifts a heavy weight ('the hammer') and allows it to fall on the head of a pile, thereby driving the pile into the ground. When the hammer has been lifted to the top, it has only to be released to fall and do work on the pile. The capacity for doing work is present in the hammer as soon as it has been lifted, simply because of its position several feet above the ground. The actual work on the pile is done at the expense of kinetic energy gained during the hammer's fall, but the capacity for working is present before the fall starts. Energy of this sort, depending merely on the position of an object, is called *potential* energy.

Potential energy

▼

4   Prior to the development of nuclear power plants, all the significant contributions to the mechanical energy used by man had the sun as their source. However, economical methods have not been developed as yet for *directly* converting solar radiation into work on a large scale. The amount of energy striking the earth from the sun is staggering when considered as a whole, but per unit surface the quantity is small. This introduces the serious difficulty of concentrating the heat gathered from a large surface and using it as a source for conversion to work. Significant research on this difficulty is underway, and progress has been made on the related problem of the use of solar energy directly as heat; for example, solar radiation is being used to heat homes, to produce high temperatures for metallurgical operations (solar furnaces), and to concentrate aqueous solutions by evaporation.

5   The kinetic energy due to the mass movement of air has been used to some extent for the production of work, especially in rural areas (windmills). Variations and uncertainties in wind velocity, and the necessity for large-sized equipment to produce significant quantities of work, are problems retarding progress in this field.

6   Conceivably, the available potential energy of tides could be concentrated and utilized. Attempts in this direction on a large scale have been made in parts of the world where tides are extreme. However, the total power production in this manner is unlikely to be highly significant in comparison with world demands for energy.

7   By far the most important sources of power are the chemical (molecular) energy of fuels, nuclear energy, and the potential energy of waterfalls. The use of water power involves the transformation of mechanical energy from one form to another; hence, 100 percent efficiency is theoretically possible. On the other hand, all present-day methods for the *large-scale* use of molecular and nuclear energy are based on the evolution of energy as heat, and subsequent conversion of part of the heat into useful work.

Accordingly, the efficiency of all such processes is destined to be low (values greater than 30 percent are uncommon), despite improvements in the design of equipment. This is, of course, a direct consequence of the second law of thermodynamics which states that heat cannot be converted into work unless some of the heat is transferred from a higher to a lower temperature.

8   If some means could be devised to convert the energy in fuels into work without the intermediate generation of heat, conversion efficiency could be considerably improved. The usual device for the direct use of chemical energy is the electrolytic cell, in which the conversion is to electrical energy. Progress has been made in developing cells which operate on hydrogen and on carbonaceous fuels such as natural gas or coal. Such *fuel cells* are already

in use to supply modest power requirements for special purposes. The efficiency of these cells ranges from 65 to 80 percent, about twice the value obtained by the conventional process of first converting the chemical energy into heat.

9 In a conventional power plant the molecular energy of the fuel is released by a combustion process. The function of the work-producing device is to convert part of the heat of combustion into mechanical energy. In a nuclear power plant the fission or fusion process releases the energy of the nucleus of the atom as heat, and then this heat is partially converted into work.

10 In one form of heat engine, the working fluid is completely enclosed and goes through a cyclical process, accomplished by vaporization and condensation. Heat is transferred to the fluid from another part of the apparatus across a physical boundary. A coal-fired power plant with steam as the working fluid is an example. Here, the combustion gases are separated from the steam by the boiler-tube walls. The *internal-combustion engine* is another form of heat engine, characterized by the direct evolution of heat within the work-producing device. Examples of this type are the Otto engine and the combustion gas turbine.

Heat engines

Smith & Van Ness, *Introduction to Chemical Engineering Thermodynamics*, pp 488–489. McGraw-Hill, 1975.

B. Check your understanding

1. Read the text again carefully, looking up in your dictionary any words you do not understand. Then answer these questions:

1. What is the relationship between energy, force and work?

2. At what point in its operation does a pile driver possess potential energy?

3. Why is it difficult to convert solar radiation into work on a large scale?

4. What device makes use of the kinetic energy in air movement?

5. Why is 100% efficiency theoretically possible with water power?

6. What is the connection between the second law of thermodynamics and the low efficiency of systems using molecular and nuclear energy?

7. Why are fuel cells more efficient for producing power than heat engines?

8. What is the relationship between energy, heat and work?

2. Now say what the words or phrases below refer to:

● this sort (paragraph 3)   ● this manner (6)
● This (4)   ● This (7)
● This difficulty (4)   ● this heat (9)
● this field (5)   ● this type (10)

3.
● Give one example of something which possesses or demonstrates kinetic energy and one example of something which demonstrates potential energy.
● Summarise the ideas given in Paragraph 7 from the line beginning: 'On the other hand . . .'
● What difference is there between the production of molecular energy in a conventional power plant compared with a nuclear power plant?

▼

C. Increase your vocabulary

Using your dictionary if necessary, complete the following exercises.

1. Say which words in the first three paragraphs have the same meaning as:

- because of
- to move
- limited
- only

2. Now do the same from paragraph 4:

- before
- changing
- collected
- in progress

3. Find alternative words with more or less the same meaning as:

- retarding (paragraph 5)
- utilized (6)
- consequence (7)
- devised (8)
- conventional (9)
- cyclical (10)

4. Give the NOUN forms of the following:

- performing
- restricted
- converting
- significant
- devised
- separated

D. Check your grammar

1. CAPACITY AND ABILITY

We can use several different verb forms or special phrases to describe the ability of something to do certain tasks. Look at the example below:

> - A hammer *can* drive a pile into the ground.
> - It *has the ability to* do the work.
> - It *has the capacity to* do the work.
> - A moving object *is capable of exerting* a force.

Use one of these ways of expressing ability and capacity to make sentences from the examples below:

- A crane .... lift heavy loads.
- A windmill .... produce power.
- A combustion engine .... convert heat into mechanical energy.
- Modern power plants .... generate thousands of watts of electric power.
- A strong support .... bear considerable loads.
- Certain alloys .... withstand extremely high temperatures.
- A Formula I racing car .... travel at over 220 mph.
- Modern aircraft .... fly long distances without refuelling.

2. 'CAUSE', 'ENABLE' AND 'ALLOW'

When we want to show how the action or ability of one thing can affect another, we can use verbs such as those shown in the example below:

- A force can *cause* an object *to shift* its position.
- Energy is the property of something that *enables* it *to do* work.
- A pile driver is a machine that lifts a hammer and then *allows* it *to fall* on the head of a pile.

Now express these ideas using one of these constructions (only one is appropriate in each case):

- The nuclear fission process   →   heat energy is released.

- New technology   →   manufacturers increase production.

- The use of satellites   →   scientists can predict the weather.

- Electron microscopes   →   we can see things only a fraction of a millimetre in size.

- Burning fossil fuels   →   the ozone layer of the Earth's atmosphere breaks down.

- The gaps in railway lines   →   the metal can expand without buckling in hot weather.

3. REPORTING ON PROGRESS

We can use different tense forms to report on progress. We can talk about what is happening at the time we speak or about what has happened up to the time we speak. Look at the examples below:

- Progress *has been made* on the use of solar energy for heating purposes.
- Further research *is underway*.
- Large scale use of solar radiation *has not been developed yet*.
- Solar radiation *is being used* to heat homes on a small scale.

Refer to the text and complete the sentences below:

(a) Tidal Power
- Attempts to develop tide power ....
- The use of tide power on a large scale ....
- Tide power .... to produce energy in experimental programs in Europe.
- Efforts to develop the potential energy of tides ....

(b) Now write four similar sentences on the topic of Wind Power.

E. Understanding a lecture

Listen to this lecture about a device which converts energy into work. Look at the incomplete notes first and try to complete them as the lecturer gives his talk. Try to complete as much as possible the first time you hear the lecture:

1. Title: Horizontal Axis ....

2. Basic design: Rotor or rotors on .... rotate
   to convert wind into power via ....
   ....

3. Rotor materials: Wood, glass reinforced plastic, ...
   ....

4. Rotor types (i) ....
   and   (ii) ....
   position (iii) Two or more sets of counter rotating blades.

5. Lift turbines: (i) Consist of .... with
                   aerofoil section to produce ....
                 (ii) Small rotors turn at ....
                 (iii) Large rotors turn at ....
                   but blade tips reach speed of ....

6. Drag turbines: (i) Blades rely on .... to get
                   energy from wind.
                 (ii) Blades turn ....
                 (iii) Not suitable for ....
                 (iv) Used for ....

7. Control techniques: (i) Rotors have .... to slow them down,
                     (ii) Rotors are made from ....
                     (iii) Most machines have .... to stop
                       rotation.

F. Understanding a printed text (2)

Read the following text carefully, looking up anything you do not understand.

Conversion of heat to work by power cycles

1 *The Otto Engine.* This is an internal combustion engine which, like others, employs a fuel mixture as the working medium, with the result that the thermal energy from the combustion process is available within the work-producing machine, for example a piston-and-cylinder assembly.

2   The internal combustion engine does not, thermodynamically speaking, strictly demonstrate a completely cyclical process since the fuel–air mixture is burned and the products of combustion are rejected to the surroundings.

3   Because of the characteristic features of the internal combustion engine, it may (1) be built as a small compact power plant suitable for nonstationary applications and (2) operate at high temperatures and therefore at relatively high efficiencies.

4   The ordinary Otto engine cycle used in automobiles consists of an intake stroke at essentially constant pressure, during which period the fuel–air mixture flows into the cylinder. During the second stroke, all valves are closed and the fuel–air mixture is compressed. The mixture is then ignited, and the combustion is so rapid with respect to the rate of piston movement that the volume remains nearly constant. Then follows the work-producing stroke, in which the high-temperature, high-pressure products of combustion expand. When the exhaust valve is opened at the end of the expansion stroke, the pressure is rapidly reduced to a value just above the exhaust pressure. This is, approximately, a constant volume process. Finally, during the exhaust stroke, the piston pushes out the combustion gases remaining in the cylinder at about constant pressure. The effect of increasing the compression ratio is to increase the efficiency of the engine, i.e. to increase the work produced per unit quantity of fuel.

5   *The Diesel Engine.* This engine differs from the Otto engine primarily in that the temperature at the end of the compression process is such that combustion is initiated spontaneously. This higher temperature is obtained by continuing the compression step to a higher pressure, or higher compression ratio. The fuel is not injected until the end of the compression process, and then it is added at such a slow rate in comparison with the rate of piston travel that the combustion process occurs, ideally, at constant pressure. In general, the Otto engine has a higher efficiency than the Diesel for a given compression ratio. However, preignition difficulties limit the compression ratio in the Otto engine, so that the higher ratios can be used in the Diesel engine, and for that reason, higher efficiencies can be obtained.

6   *The Combustion-Gas-Turbine Power Plant.* Consideration of the Otto and Diesel engines has shown that direct utilization of the energy of high-temperature and high-pressure gases, without external transfer of heat, possesses some advantages in power production.

7   On the other hand, the turbine is more efficient in utilizing this energy than the reciprocating piston, primarily because of the friction accompanying the continual reversal of direction of the piston and friction in the valve operations. The combustion gas turbine is the result of attempts to combine in one unit the advantages of internal combustion and the turbine.

8   The gas turbine utilizes high-temperature gases from the combustion space to operate an expansion turbine, as indicated in Fig. 11–6. To obtain high efficiencies the air must be compressed (supercharged) to several atmospheres pressure before combustion, just as it is in the internal-combustion piston engine. By employing a centrifugal compressor, the turbine and compressor may operate on the same shaft (Fig. 11–6), with part of the work from the turbine used to drive the compressor. The unit shown in Fig. 11–6 is a complete power plant, as is an Otto or Diesel engine.

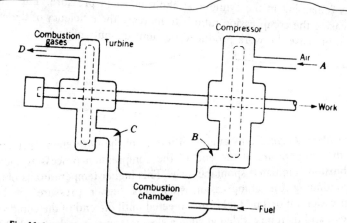

Fig. 11-6 *Combustion-gas-turbine power plant.*

9   *Jet Engines, Jet-Propulsion Cycles.* In the power cycles considered up to this point the high-temperature, high-pressure gas has been expanded in a turbine (steam power plant, gas turbine) or a reciprocating piston-and-cylinder assembly (Otto and Diesel cycles). In either case, the power has been available in the form of a rotating shaft. Another device for expanding the hot gases is a jet or nozzle. Here the power is available in the kinetic energy of the exhaust gases leaving the apparatus. The entire power plant, consisting of a compression device and a combustion chamber, as well as a jet, is known as a jet engine. Since the kinetic energy of the exhaust gases is directly available for propelling the engine and its attachments, such systems are most commonly used for aircraft propulsion. There are several types of jet-propulsion engines based on different ways of accomplishing the compression and expansion processes. Since the air striking the engine has kinetic energy (with respect to the engine), its pressure may be increased in a diffuser.

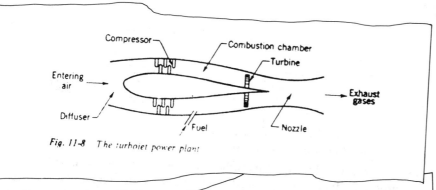

Fig. 11-8 The turbojet power plant.

10   The turbojet engine illustrated in Fig. 11–8 takes advantage of a diffuser to reduce the work of the compressor. The axial-flow compressor completes the job of compression, and then the fuel is introduced and burned in the combustion chamber. The hot combustion gases first pass through a turbine where the expansion is just sufficient to provide enough power to drive the compressor. The remainder of the expansion to the exhaust pressure is accomplished in the nozzle. Here, the velocity of the gases with respect to the engine is increased to a level above that of the entering air. This increase in velocity provides a thrust (force) on the engine in the forward direction.

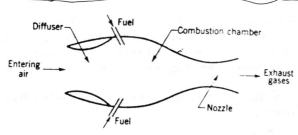

Fig. 11-9 The ram-jet power plant.

11   If the compression in the diffuser can be carried to a high enough pressure, an efficient engine can be obtained without a compressor. Under these conditions, the entire expansion process is accomplished in the exhaust nozzle, and all the energy output is in the kinetic energy of the exhaust gases. This type of engine (Fig. 11–9) is known as a ram jet. In order to obtain a high pressure at the exit of the diffuser, the entrance velocity (with respect to the engine) must be high. Ram-jet engines do not have an efficiency comparable to that of turbojets unless the engine is moving in the atmosphere at supersonic velocities.

12   *Rocket Engines.* A rocket engine differs from the turbojet and ram-jet power plants in that the oxidizing agent is carried with the engine. Instead of depending on the surrounding air for burning the fuel, the rocket is self-contained. This means that the rocket will operate in a vacuum such as outer space. In fact, the performance will be better in a vacuum, because none of the thrust is required to overcome frictional forces.

▼

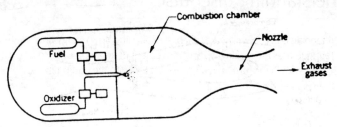

Fig. 11-10   Liquid rocket engine.

13   In rockets using liquid fuels the oxidizing agent (such as liquid oxygen, nitric acid, fluorine) is pumped from tanks into the combustion chamber. Simultaneously, fuel (such as aniline, ethanol, petroleum fractions known as JP fuels, hydrazine) is pumped into the chamber and burned. The combustion takes place at constant pressure and produces high-temperature exhaust gases. These are then expanded through a nozzle as indicated in Fig. 11–10.

Ibid: pp 497–509.

G. Check your understanding

1. The Otto Engine

- What does the Otto engine have in common with other internal combustion engines?
- Why doesn't the internal combustion engine demonstrate a completely cyclical process?
- What are the names of the four strokes of the ordinary Otto engine cycle?
- What is the connection between compression ratio and engine efficiency?

2. Make a list of the differences between the Otto and Diesel engines. Write them down under two headings:

Otto	**Diesel**

3. There are three similarities mentioned between the Otto and Diesel engines and the Gas Turbine. What are they?

4. Jet Engines

- Try to explain the sentence below, using your own words as much as possible:

  'Here the power is available in the kinetic energy of the exhaust gases leaving the apparatus.' (paragraph 9)
- In the turbojet engine, what is the function of the diffuser?
- How does a ram-jet differ from a turbo-jet?

5. Rocket Engines

- How can a rocket engine operate in a vacuum such as outer space?
- Explain the relationship between oxidizing agent, fuel combustion chamber and nozzle in the jet engine.

6. Choose TWO of the engine types you have just read about. Using your answers to the questions and your own notes, try to prepare a short summary of either the differences or the similarities between the engines.

H. Understanding discourse

Listen to your tape again. You will hear someone explaining how energy changes from one form to another. He uses the starting-up and movement of an automobile to give examples. As you listen, write down the form of energy associated with the equipment shown below and the process the speaker describes.

1. Complete the diagram:

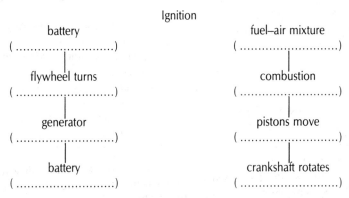

Ignition

battery
(.........................)

flywheel turns
(.........................)

generator
(.........................)

battery
(.........................)

fuel–air mixture
(.........................)

combustion
(.........................)

pistons move
(.........................)

crankshaft rotates
(.........................)

2. Listen to your tape again and look at the sentences below which are in note form. First, put the sentences (which you should number from 1 to 7) in their correct order and then write complete sentences from the notes to give the description of energy changes.

.... Then, chemical energy/fuel and air/to heat energy/ignition.
.... Most forms of energy/converted/other forms.
.... Next, mechanical energy/piston movement causes/crankshaft/rotate. As a result,/ wheels turn.
.... First, ignition switched on/electrical energy/battery/to mechanical energy/turn flywheel.
.... Good example/automobile engine and movement.
.... Almost immediately, heat energy/to mechanical energy/expanding gases/pistons down.
.... All the time, mechanical energy/to turn generator. This/electrical energy/charge battery.

CONTROL DEVICES

A. Understanding a printed text (1)

The following text will introduce you to the topic of **control devices** — in this case, valves. As usual, pay attention to the section headings and the paragraph information. Remember that the notes at the side will help you to refer quickly to the most important facts. Look also at the diagrams and captions.

Now look at these questions and read through the text to find the answers.

Remember, you do not have to understand all the words to answer them.

1. What type of valve is not included in the text?
2. How many types of pipe valves are discussed?
3. Are all valves made from the same materials?
4. How are hydraulic turbine valves usually operated?
5. How do compressor and pump valves usually operate?

Valves

1 *Definition.* A valve is a flow-control device. This text deals with valves for fluids, liquids and gases. Valves are used to regulate the flow of fluids in piping systems and machinery. In machinery the flow phenomenon is frequently of a pulsating or intermittent character and the valve, with its associated gear, contributes a timing feature. This particular text does not deal with electrical valves.

Different types of valves have different functions

2 *Types of valves.* There are many different types of valves in operation — each designed to perform a specific function. This section will consider some types from the point of view of design, construction and function.

3   Four particular valve types are commonly used in piping systems. Each is illustrated below and each has its own distinctive features and applications. Gate valves are usually operated closed or wide open. They are seldom used for throttling, i.e. regulating flow, to any fine degree. Globe valves, on the other hand, are adaptable to throttling operations and are often fitted with a renewable disk. Check valves are used for limiting flow automatically to a single direction in a piping system while plug valves operate in the open or closed position by turning the plug through 90° with a shearing action. This enables it to clear foreign matter from the seat.

Valves have different design features and functions

Check valves

Plug valves

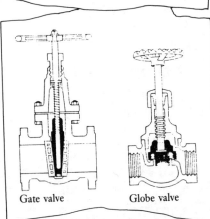

Gate valve   Globe valve

4   *Valve features and materials.* Some of the most common structural features of pipe valves are: outside stem and yoke, packless construction; angle, as opposed to straightway flow; power instead of manual operation; and combined non-return and stop-valve arrangements.

5   These valves may also be made from a variety of materials, depending upon their particular function and the stress they undergo during operation. Brass and bronze are usual in valves for general service. Cast iron may be used where there are low steam pressures (less than 250 psi) and temperatures, or hydraulic pressures, below 800 psi. However, steel and alloy steels are required for the highest operating pressures such as 5000 psi and 1200°F steam. Where there are chemical and process applications, special metals must be used.

Types of metal used in valves

6   *Safety and relief valves.* A word now about safety and relief valves which are automatic protection devices for the relief of excess pressure. They must open automatically when the pressure exceeds a predetermined value and they must allow the pressure to drop a predetermined amount before closing to avoid chattering, instability and damage to the valve and valve seat. They must have adjustment features for both the relieving and blowdown pressures and, finally, they must be tamperproof after setting.

Valves which operate for safety purposes

7   *Hydraulic turbine valves.* Obviously these are used for hydraulic turbines and hydroelectric systems. The purpose of the valves and gates in these systems is to control water flow for (1) regulation of power output at sustained efficiency and with minimum wastage of water and (2) safety under the inertial flow conditions of large masses of water. Valve sizes are usually large, for example, 6 feet in diameter, so that power operation is necessary. The valves come in various types, such as gate, butterfly and needle — the last two of which are shown below.

Some features of valves which control water flow

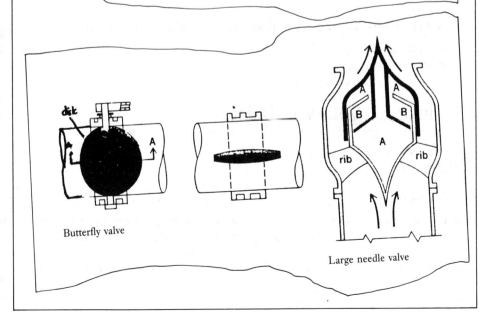

Butterfly valve

Large needle valve

8   *Compressor and pump valves.* In compressors, valves are usually automatic, operating by pressure difference (<5 psi) on the two sides of a moveable, spring-loaded member and without any mechanical linkage to the moving parts of the compressor mechanism. Valves here have to tolerate and handle air speeds to the order of 5000 ft/min. Where pressure is greater than 1000 psi, the normal plate valve is replaced by automatic poppet valves to give greater strength and tightness under loading.

9   Like those for compressors, pump valves are usually of the automatic type operating by pressure differences. However, working conditions are very different because liquids are handled and the valves therefore have to be capable of dealing with entrained solids, corrosive chemicals, high viscosity and so on. Fluid speeds are low (200–300 ft/min) with cold water and 100 ft/min with viscous liquids when compared with compressors.

Encyclopedia of Science and Technology, pp 290–293. McGraw-Hill, 1971.

B. Check your understanding

1. Now read the text carefully and try to answer these questions:

1. What do you understand by the phrase 'the flow of fluids'?

2. What is a special feature of the plug valve?

3. What factors determine the material used for valves?

4. What is the main function of safety and relief valves?

5. Why are hydraulic turbine valves power-operated?

6. What feature do compressor and pump valves have in common?

7. Under what conditions do poppet valves replace plate valves?

2. Now try to complete these definitions using the information given in the text. Look at the example below:

- A check valve is a valve which allows fluid to flow in only one direction.

- A gate valve is a valve ....
- Safety valves are used to ....
- Automatic valves operate ....

C. Increase your vocabulary

Remember to use your dictionary where necessary in this section:

1. In paragraph 1:

- What word means 'to control'?
- Which word means 'stopping and starting again'?
- Which word could you replace with 'equipment'?

2. In paragraphs 2 and 3:

- What words also mean 'a particular job'?
- How is the phrase 'that is to say' expressed here?
- How would you explain 'foreign matter'?

3. Opposites

Find words in the text which have opposite meanings to those below:

- often
- automatic
- maximum
- unusual
- to allow
- fixed

4. New words

Use your dictionary to find the meanings of:

- to shear
- predetermined
- to chatter
- inertia
- corrosive
- viscosity

5. Nouns

Find the nouns in the text which relate to these verbs:

- to devise
- to apply
- to vary
- to waste
- to tighten
- to link

D. Check your grammar

1. INFINITIVE OR GERUND?

> **Remember:**
> - Computers *enable* us *to carry out* complex calculations.
> - Filters are *used to remove* contaminants from fluids.
> - Lubricants *prevent* moving parts *from overheating*.

Choose the correct form in each of the sentences below.

- Valves are used *to regulate* the flow of fluids.
              regulating

- Safety valves prevent pressure from *to exceed* safe limits.
                      exceeding

- The valve allows the pressure *to drop* a set amount before closing.
                  dropping

- Workers should avoid *to wear* loose clothing near machines.
              wearing

- Check valves are used for *to limit* flow to a single direction in a piping system.
              limiting

- A micrometer enables engineers *to measure* diameters with great accuracy.
                  measuring

- The engine stopped *to work* because of a blocked fuel line.
              working

- Students are prohibited *to smoke* in the classroom.
              from smoking

- Students are permitted *to bring* calculators into the examination room.
              from bringing

- This experiment is intended *to show* the effects of heat on metal.
              showing

▼

> **Notice how we can explain a noun compound:**
> - A *flow-control device* is a piece of equipment which controls the movement of fluids.
> - A *spring-loaded member* is a part which operates by means of the action of a spring.

(a) Write similar definitions of the following:

- a fuel-injection engine
- carbon-steel brakes
- high-velocity steam
- a three-pin plug
- a four-stroke engine cycle

(b) What noun compounds can be made to describe the following?

- A system which allows traffic to travel in one direction only.

- An aircraft engine which operates by means of a turbine driving a propeller.

- A mixture which is a combination of air and fuel, usually needed in automotive engines.

- A piece of electrical equipment which can play two cassettes in stereo.

- A tall building of eight storeys which is divided into apartments.

E. Understanding a lecture

On your tape you can hear part of a lecture. Complete the tasks given by the speaker and also answer the questions below. They are divided into sections corresponding to the sections of the lecture.

Section 1

1. Is this the first information the students have had about valves?
2. What three effects do valves have on flow?
3. Why do the diagrams contain no information at all?

Section 2

Complete Diagram 1 with the words, signs and arrows according to the instructions given by the speaker.

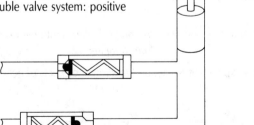

Diagram 1. Double valve system: positive pressure

Complete Diagram 2 with the words, signs
and arrows as you did for the previous
diagram.

Diagram 2. Double valve system: negative
pressure

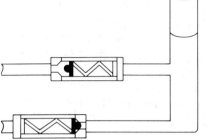

Section 4

Add the necessary information to Diagram 3
according to the speaker's instructions.

Diagram 3

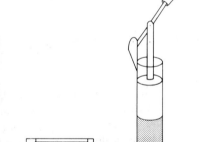

Section 5

1. What does the fluid in the work cylinder
   do?
2. Why can't the check valves be used to
   lower the work piston?
3. What happens when the release valve is
   opened?

Description of operation
Now listen again to the section about the
system with the release valve. Use the facts
you hear as well as the diagram to prepare a
description of how the work piston is raised
and lowered in this system.

F. Understanding a printed text (2)

Read the following text carefully, looking up anything you do not understand.

Internal Combustion Engine Valves and Valve Train

1   Poppet valves are used almost exclusively in internal combustion reciprocation engines because of the demands for tightness with high operating temperatures and pressures. The valves (see illustration below) are generally 2 inches in diameter or smaller on high-speed automotive-type engines. They are cam-operated and spring-loaded. They are cooled by transferring heat to the engine jacket, mostly through the valve stem. Exhaust valves are subject to the effects of extreme temperature and must accordingly be most carefully designed and constructed of alloy metals.

Diagram 1

Poppet valve for internal combustion engine.

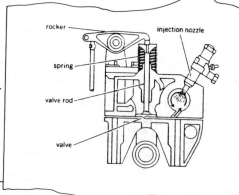

2   By valve train, we mean the valves and valve-operating mechanism by which an internal combustion engine takes air or a fuel–air mixture into the cylinders and discharges the combustion products to the exhaust. Mechanically, an internal combustion engine is a reciprocating pump, able to draw in a certain amount of air per minute. Since the fuel takes up little space but needs air with which to combine, the power output of an engine is limited by its air-pumping capacity.

3   It is essential that the flow through the engine be restricted as little as possible. This is the first requirement for valves. The second is that they close off the cylinder during the compression and power strokes.

4   In most 4-stroke engines, the valves are of the inward-opening poppet type, with the valve head ground to fit a conical seat in the cylinder block or cylinder head.

5   The valve head is held concentric with its seat by a cylindrical stem running in the valve guide. The valve is held closed by a compressed helical spring. The valve is opened wide by lifting it from its seat a distance equal to approximately 25% of the valve diameter. Valves are usually made of a stainless, non-scaling alloy which will keep its strengthened shape at high temperature. Exhaust valves sometimes are made hollow and partially filled with metallic sodium to permit more effective cooling.

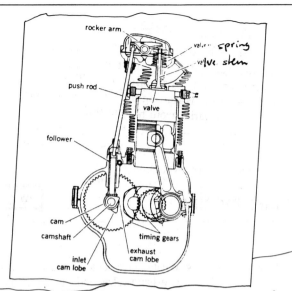

rocker arm

valve spring

valve stem

push rod

valve

follower

cam

camshaft

timing gears

exhaust cam lobe

inlet cam lobe

Diagram 2

6   Engine valves are usually opened by means of cams. The diagram below illustrates the typical construction and operation of the cam as it causes the valve to open.

7   Riding on each cam is a follower or valve-lifter, which may be a flat or slightly convex surface, or a roller. The valve is opened by forces applied to the end of the valve stem through a mechanical linkage activated by the cam follower. The diagram shows the camshaft placed in the crankcase, which is usual in standard automobiles. The operating linkage consists of cam follower, push rod and rocker arm. The push rod is a light rod or tube with ball ends which carries the motion of the cam follower to the rocker arm. The rocker arm is a lever, pivoted near its centre so that as the push rod raises one end, the other end depresses the valve stem, opening the valve.

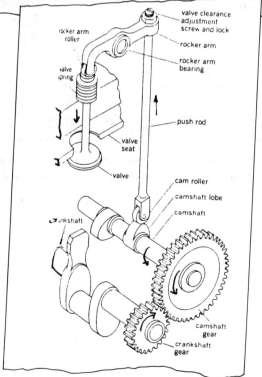

valve clearance adjustment screw and lock

rocker arm roller

rocker arm

rocker arm bearing

valve spring

push rod

valve seat

valve

cam roller

camshaft lobe

camshaft

crankshaft

camshaft gear

crankshaft gear

Diagram 3

8   To ensure tight closing of the valve even when the valve stem lengthens from thermal expansion, the valve train is adjusted to provide some clearance when the follower is on the low part of the cam. The cam shape includes a ramp which reduces shock by starting the lift at about 2 feet per second, even though the clearance varies from time to time.

Encyclopedia of Science and Technology, pp 290–293. McGraw-Hill, 1971.

G. Check your understanding

1. In the first paragraph:

- What word can mean 'without exception'?
- Can you find a word which can mean 'usually'?
- What is the word which means 'because of this fact'?

2. In paragraphs 2 and 3:

- Give your own definition of 'valve train'.
- What can limit the power output of an engine?
- What is the secondary function of valves in an internal combustion engine?

3. In paragraphs 4 and 5:

- What shape is the valve stem?
- What is the name of the device which keeps the valve closed?

- What is the function of metallic sodium in exhaust valves and where is it to be found?

4. From Diagram 3:

- How is the cam follower connected to the rocker arm?
- What happens when the camshaft lobe meets the cam roller?
- What causes the camshaft gear to rotate?

5. Describe orally the complete sequence of actions involved in the opening and closing of a valve, as shown in the third diagram. Try to explain using the passive form of verbs, e.g.:
First, the camshaft gear *is rotated* by the crankshaft.

H. Understanding discourse

A student is asking his friend questions after a lecture. He is not sure of his notes and wants to check details. Listen to the conversation and write down the FOUR questions he asks.

1. _____? (Clarification)
2. _____? (Spelling)
3. _____? (Meaning)
4. _____? (Explanation)

The following text will help you to check how well you are learning the skills you will need when studying engineering in English.

A. Reading

Read the following text and then answer the questions.

Compressors in refrigeration and air conditioning

1   Each of the four components of a vapor-compression system — the compressor, the condenser, the expansion device and the evaporator — has its own peculiar behavior. At the same time, each component is influenced by conditions imposed by the other members of the quartet. A change in condenser-water temperature, for example, may change the rate of refrigerant to the compressor pumps, which, in turn, may require the expansion valve to readjust and the refrigerant in the evaporator to change pressure. However, the heart of the vapor-compression system is the compressor.

2   The four most common types of refrigeration compressors are the reciprocating, screw, centrifugal and vane. The reciprocating compressor consists of a piston moving back and forth in a cylinder with suction and discharge valves arranged to allow pumping to take place. The screw, centrifugal and vane compressors all use rotating elements. The screw and vane compressors are positive-displacement machines and the centrifugal compressor operates by virtue of centrifugal force.

3   The workhorse of the refrigeration industry is the reciprocating compressor, built in sizes ranging from fractional-kilowatt to hundreds of kilowatts refrigeration capacity. Modern compressors are single-acting and may be single-cylinder or multi-cylinder. In multi-cylinder compressors, the cylinders are in V, W, radial or in-line arrangements.

4   During the suction stroke of the piston, low-pressure gas is drawn in through the suction valve, which may be located in the piston or in the head. During the discharge stroke, the piston compresses the refrigerant and then pushes it out through the discharge valve, which is usually located in the cylinder head. Following the trend of most rotative machinery, the operating speed of compressors has generally increased in the past 20 years. From the slow speeds of early compressors of about 2 or 3 r/s, the speeds have increased until compressors today operate at speeds as high as 60 r/s.

5   A compressor whose crankshaft extends through the compressor housing so that the motor can be externally coupled to a shaft is called an open-type compressor. A seal must be used where the shaft comes through the compressor housing to prevent refrigerant gas from leaking out or air from leaking in if the crankcase pressure is lower than atmospheric. Even though designers have continually developed better seals, piercing in the housing always represents a source of leakage. To avoid leakage, the motor and compressor are often enclosed in the same housing.

6   Improved techniques for insulating the motor electrically have allowed motors to operate even though they are in contact with the refrigerant. In many designs the cold suction gas is drawn across the motor to keep it cool. Almost all small motor-compressor combinations are used in refrigerators, freezers and residential air-conditioners are of the hermetic type. The only connections to the compressor housing are the suction and discharge fittings and electric terminals. Moisture in the system can be damaging to the motor; therefore, dehydration of hermetic units before charging is essential.

Answer these questions.

1. The operation of each component in the vapour-compression cycle

(a) is unusual. ☐
(b) affects the operation of the other components. ☐
(c) does not affect other components' operation. ☐
(d) affects the compressor. ☐

2. The four types of refrigeration compressor can be classified as

(a) all the same. ☐
(b) all different. ☐
(c) three similar and one different. ☐
(d) three different and one similar. ☐

3. Reciprocating compressors have

(a) a very small refrigeration capacity. ☐
(b) a very large refrigeration capacity. ☐
(c) a wide refrigeration capacity. ☐
(d) an unknown refrigeration capacity. ☐

4. The suction valve is located

(a) in the piston. ☐
(b) in the head. ☐
(c) in either the piston or the head. ☐
(d) in the refrigerant. ☐

5. Which of these statements is correct?

(a) Seals are necessary to stop gas escaping and air entering. ☐
(b) Seals are necessary to stop air escaping and gas entering. ☐

6. Is this statement correct or incorrect?

Leakage in compressors is difficult to prevent.
        correct ☐ incorrect ☐

7. 'Dehydration' (paragraph 6) means

(a) removing water from something ☐
(b) adding water to something ☐
(c) disconnecting something ☐
(d) insulating something ☐

8. Another way of expressing 'to avoid' (paragraph 5) is to use

(a) to allow ☐
(b) to reduce ☐
(c) to prevent ☐
(d) to control ☐

9. The most important component of the vapour-compression system is

(a) the compressor ☐
(b) the condenser ☐
(c) the expansion device ☐
(d) the evaporator ☐

10. Compressor speeds in the last 20 years

(a) remained the same ☐
(b) increased rapidly ☐
(c) increased greatly ☐
(d) increased slowly ☐

B. Writing

Read the information below on types of power systems available for water pumping stations. Use any of the facts to write a paragraph describing the differences between any TWO types.

Then write a paragraph explaining which system you would select for your city. Think about the size of the city, the cost of fuel, etc.

	FOR	AGAINST
Steam Boilers	• good for large plants • reliable • simple	• requires cheap fuel supply
Steam Turbines	• requires small space • simple to use • reliable	• needs connection to centrifugal pump • also needs reducing gears
Diesel Engines	• good fuel economy • good for medium size plants • self-contained system	• expensive to install • needs skilled maintenance • noisy
Gasoline Engines	• cheap to install • no need for reducing gears • good for standby or emergency	• high operating cost • needs batteries to start — constant electrical supply
Electric	• electricity is available in off-peak hours • provides good drive for centrifugal pump • simple construction • reliable and strong	• electricity may not always be cheap • very large and heavy

C. Listening

You will now hear part of a lecture. You will hear each section of the lecture twice. After you have listened to each section for the second time, answer the questions below.

Section 1

1. Gasoline engine components are

(a) lighter than diesel engine components. ☐
(b) heavier than diesel engine components. ☐
(c) much lighter than diesel engine components. ☐
(d) much heavier than diesel engine components. ☐

▼

51

2. The compression ratio in diesel engines can be as high as

    (a) 14:1   (b) 24:1   (c) 42:1   (d) 41:1

3. Diesel engines are not self-speed limiting because

    (a) they have no manual control.   ☐
    (b) there is no valve in the carburettor.   ☐
    (c) the amount of air available for combustion is unlimited.   ☐
    (d) they can accelerate very fast.   ☐

4. Diesel engines can accelerate at a rate of

    (a) 2000 rev/s   ☐
    (b) 200 revs/s   ☐
    (c) 2000 rpm   ☐
    (d) 200 rpm   ☐

5. Is this statement correct or incorrect?

    A diesel engine does not have an ignition system.
          correct ☐   incorrect ☐

Section 2———————————————————————

1. The diesel engine converts

    (a) mechanical energy to heat energy.   ☐
    (b) compression ratio to mechanical energy.   ☐
    (c) fuel to energy.   ☐
    (d) heat energy in fuel to mechanical energy.   ☐

2. On the diagrams below, indicate BDC, TDC and write down the compression ratio.

(a)   (b)

Compression ratio = _____

3. A four-stroke engine cycle requires the crankshaft to turn through

    (a) 72° to complete one working cycle.   ☐

    (b) 720° to complete one working cycle.   ☐

    (c) 172° to complete one working cycle.   ☐

    (d) 360° to complete one working cycle.   ☐

4. Below each diagram, write down the name of each stroke needed for one working cycle of a four-stroke engine.

 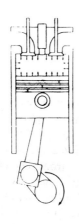 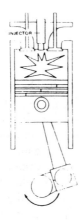 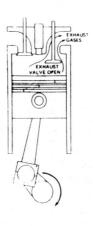

1 _____   2 _____   3 _____   4 _____

PUMPS

A. Understanding a printed text (1)

This passage introduces you to the different **types of pumps** and the characteristics of each type.

As you read, look for the answers to the following questions. Remember, you do not have to understand all the words to answer the questions.

1. What feature is common to all centrifugal pumps?
2. How does the axial-flow pump differ from the centrifugal pump?
3. How many different kinds of pumps are named?

Centrifugal and axial-flow pumps

DEFINITIONS

The centrifugal pump is so called because the pressure increase within its rotor due to centrifugal action is an important factor in its operation. In brief, it consists of an impeller rotating within a case as in Figure 1 below. Fluid enters the impeller in the center portion, called the eye, flows outwardly, and is discharged around the entire circumference into a casing. During flow through the rotating impeller the fluid receives energy from the vanes, resulting in an increase in both pressure and absolute velocity. Since a large part of the energy of the fluid leaving the impeller is kinetic, it is necessary to reduce the absolute velocity and transform the large portion of this velocity head into pressure head. This is accomplished in the volute casing surrounding the impeller (Figure 1) or in the flow through the diffuser vanes (Figure 2).

The demand for greater capacity, without increasing the diameter to obtain it, resulted in an increase in the dimensions parallel to the shaft. This in turn required an increase in the eye diameter to accommodate the larger flow and a corresponding change in the vanes at entrance, resulting in the mixed-flow impeller whose specific speed is higher than that of a radial-flow impeller.

A still further increase in specific speed is obtained with the propeller, or axial-flow pump. In this type there is no change in radius of a given streamline, and hence centrifugal action plays no part.

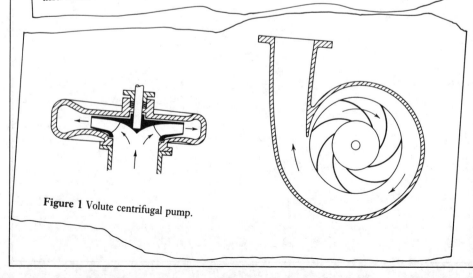

Figure 1 Volute centrifugal pump.

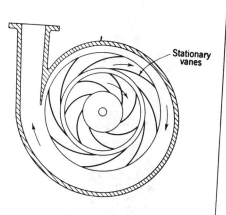

Figure 2 Diffuser (or turbine) pump. This type of pump is not typical of modern practice and would be found only in large pumps where the diffuser vanes are needed for structural reasons. In modern turbine pumps the diffuser vanes are three-dimensional as in Fig. 3 and cannot readily be shown in a drawing.

CLASSIFICATION

Centrifugal pumps are divided into two general classes: 1) volute pumps and 2) diffuser or turbine pumps. In <u>the former</u> the impeller is surrounded by a spiral case as in Figure 1, the outer boundary of which may be a curve called a volute. The absolute velocity of the fluid leaving the impeller is reduced in the volute casing, with a resultant increase in pressure. In the diffuser pump, shown in Figure 2, the impeller is surrounded by diffuser vanes which provide gradually enlarging passages to bring about a gradual reduction in velocity. Because of the superficial resemblance to a reaction turbine, this type is often called a turbine pump. However, it is still a centrifugal pump. These diffusion vanes are usually fixed or immovable, but in a very few instances they have been pivoted like the guide vanes in a turbine in order that the angle might be changed to conform to conditions with different rates of flow.

Centrifugal pumps are also divided into single-suction pumps and double-suction pumps. <u>The latter</u> have the advantage of symmetry, which ideally should eliminate end thrust. They also provide a larger inlet area with lower intake velocities than would be possible with a single-suction pump of the same outside diameter of the impeller.

All types of pumps may be single-stage or multistage. With the <u>latter</u>, two or more identical impellers are arranged in series, usually on a vertical shaft. The quantity of flow is the same as for one alone but the total head developed by the unit is the product of the head of one stage times the number of stages.

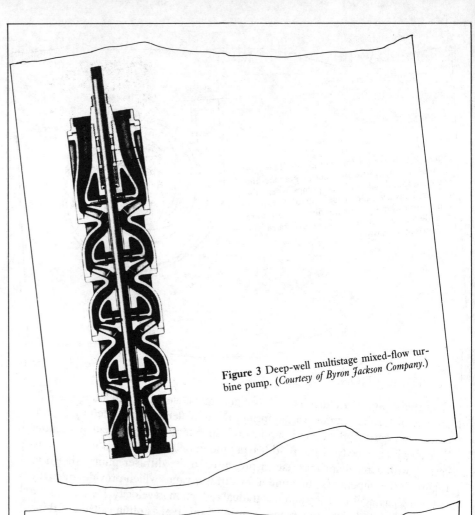

Figure 3 Deep-well multistage mixed-flow turbine pump. (*Courtesy of Byron Jackson Company.*)

A very special type is the deep-well pump of Figure 3. Since this must be installed in a well-casing of limited size, the total diameter of the pump assembly must be relatively small, and thus the impellers are even smaller in diameter. Because of the small diameter of the impeller, the head developed is not very great in one stage, and so for a deep well it is necessary to have a number of stages in order to lift the water to the desired height.

Since the casings of the deep-well pump are usually concentric and not volutes and the water must be led from the discharge from one impeller into the eye of the next, it is customary to employ diffusion vanes in the intervening passages.

Impellers can be of either the *shrouded* type, or they can be *open* or *unshrouded*. With the unshrouded impeller, the casing forms one boundary wall for the rotor passage, which necessitates the vanes having a small clearance with the casing. By contrast, the shrouded impeller has rotor passages which are completely enclosed. Open impellers are used where the material being pumped is likely to clog the passages of a shrouded impeller.

Daugherty, Franzini & Finnemore, *Fluid Mechanics with Engineering Applications*, pp 537–540. McGraw-Hill, 1985.

B. Check your understanding

Now study the text carefully. As you do, look for the answers to these questions.

1. Check these definitions to see if they are correct according to the text:

   - A centrifugal pump contains an impeller which rotates within a case.
   - The propeller pump incorporates centrifugal action.
   - Pumps which obtain a higher specific speed through the action of a propeller are called axial-flow pumps.
   - The eye is the centre portion of the impeller.
   - The diameter of the eye is smaller in the mixed-flow pump.

2. (a) Make notes or draw diagrams to help you remember how the different types of pumps are classified.

(b) Now tick all the following which are correct statements according to the text:

   - Volute pumps are centrifugal. ☐
   - Single-state pumps belong to the axial-flow type. ☐
   - Single-suction pumps belong to the centrifugal type. ☐
   - A turbine pump is a kind of centrifugal pump. ☐
   - Deep-well pumps are volutes. ☐
   - Deep-well pumps are single-state. ☐
   - Pumps with two or more impellers are called double-stage. ☐
   - Pumps with only one impeller are called single-stage. ☐

3. <u>Former</u> and <u>latter</u>. These words are underlined in the text.

   - What does the word 'former' refer to in the text?
   - What does the first example of the word 'latter' refer to?
   - What does the second example of the word 'latter' refer to?

C. Increase your vocabulary

1. Use a dictionary if necessary to make sure you know the meaning of these words and phrases used in the text:

   - in brief ● gradually ● enlarging
   - fixed ● eliminate
   - identical ● lift ● employ
   - enclosed ● clog
   - in detail
   - flow freely

2. Find the words in this list which mean the same as:

   - (to) use
   - raise
   - the same
   - stationary
   - (to) cut out

3. Find the words which mean the opposite of these:

   - reducing
   - rapidly
   - open

4. Use one of these words or phrases taken from the text in the appropriate sentences below:

   - in turn ● still further ● relatively
   - superficial ● accommodate

   1. The diffuser pump looks like a turbine, but the similarity is only _____.
   2. The total diameter of a deep-well pump must be small so that the well casing can _____ it.
   3. The use of a propeller has the effect of increasing speed _____.
   4. Double-suction pumps have a _____ large intake area so that the intake velocity is reduced.
   5. In multi-stage pumps, the water is led from the discharge of each impeller _____ until the final stage is reached.

5. Increase and reduce

Refer to the text and write the correct form of *increase* or *reduce* in each of the following sentences:

1. The centrifugal action in a pump _____ both pressure and absolute velocity.
2. It is important to _____ the absolute velocity and transform a portion of it into pressure head.
3. In order to accommodate _____ flow, the eye diameter of the pump had to be _____.

4. The diffuser vanes of a diffuser pump have the effect of _____ velocity.
5. Double-suction pumps have a larger inlet area which results in the _____ of intake velocity.
6. Because of the limited size of a well casing, the diameter of deep-well pumps must be _____.
7. The volute casing of a volute pump _____ the absolute velocity of the fluid leaving the impeller and this results in an _____ in pressure.

D. Check your grammar

1. PROCESS DESCRIPTION

> Notice how the process of the pump is described in the text:
>
> Fluid *enters* the impeller in the center portion . . . *flows* outwardly, and *is discharged* around the entire circumference into a casing.
>
> Notice the use of the *present simple* tense of the verb.

> **Remember** also the use of time-linkers, as in these sentences:
>
> - *During* flow through the rotating impeller, the fluid receives energy from the vanes.
> - *At the same time* the deflector is withdrawn from the jet.
> - *Then* the needle can be moved to increase the flow in the pipe.
> - *After* it leaves the discharge of one impeller, the water flows to the eye of the next.

Now expand these notes to produce a description of the action of a jet on a runner or wheel. Begin each sentence with one of the time-linkers given. (You can refer to the figüre.)

- First ● When ● As ● At the same time ● At first

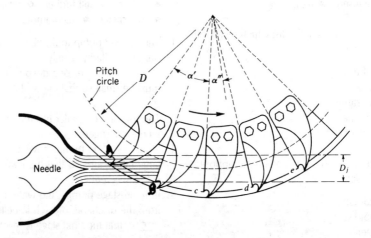

1. bucket / intercept jet / at A
2. bucket / move / towards B / more of jet / intercept
3. tip of bucket / reach B / entire jet / intercept
4. direction of bucket / downward
5. jet / push / buckets in upward direction / wheel / rotate

2. EFFECT AND RESULT

Notice how effect and result are expressed in the text:

The fluid receives energy
from the vanes   ⟶ resulting in ⟶ an increase in
                                         pressure and velocity

The demand for greater
capacity   ⟶ resulted in ⟶ an increase in
                                          dimensions

The diffuser vanes
surrounding the impeller ⟶ bring about ⟶ a gradual reduction
                                          in velocity

Now find a suitable way to express each of these ideas:
1. The pressure of water
   from the jet   ⟶   the rotation of the
                                wheel

2. Centrifugal action   ⟶   greater pressure at
                                the wall of the pipe

3. The rise in water pressure   ⟶   need for a very strong pipe

4. Reducing the power of
   the jet   ⟶   the wheel rotating
                                more slowly

5. Variations in speed   ⟶   loss of efficiency

6. Inadequate safety
   precautions   ⟶   the accident

E. Understanding a lecture

You will hear part of a lecture. It has been divided into sections to enable you to understand it more easily. As you listen, take notes. Then use your notes to answer the following questions and complete the table below.

Section 1

- Why is it important to choose the right pump for a particular situation?
- What are some of the characteristics which can vary with different types of pumps?
- What happens when you change the speed of operation of a pump?

▼

- If more than one pump is installed to carry out a single operation, we say that the pumps are installed ... or ....
- What must you make sure about if more than one pump is used for the same operation?
- What four things can happen if you don't make sure of this point?
- What word is used here which means the opposite of 'help'?

Section 2————————————————————————————————————

- What is special about the pumps at Palos Verdes?
- Complete the table below. Write in all the missing facts and figures. If any facts or figures are not given, just put a X in the space in the table.

Name of project	No. of stages	Impeller diameter	Cu.ft./sec delivered	Height in feet	Revs /min	Efficiency
Edmonton Pumping Plant						
Rocky River						

F. Understanding a printed text (2)

Read the following passage.

1.2 Distinction between a solid and a fluid

The molecules of a solid are closer together than those of a fluid. The attractive forces between the molecules of a solid are so large that a solid tends to retain its shape. This is not the case for a fluid, where the attractive forces between the molecules are smaller. There are plastic solids which flow under the proper circumstances, and even metals may flow under high pressures. On the other hand, there are certain very viscous liquids which do not flow readily, and it is easy to confuse them with the plastic solids. The distinction is that any fluid, no matter how viscous, will yield in time to the slightest stress. But a solid, no matter how plastic, requires a certain magnitude of stress to be exerted before it will flow.

Also, when the shape of a solid is altered by external forces, the tangential stresses between adjacent particles tend to restore the body to its original configuration. With a fluid, these tangential stresses depend on the velocity of deformation and vanish as the velocity approaches zero. When motion ceases, the tangential stresses disappear and the fluid does not tend to regain its original shape.

1.3 Distinction between a gas and a liquid

A fluid may be either a gas or a liquid. The molecules of gas are much farther apart than those of a liquid. Hence a gas is very compressible, and when all external pressure is removed, it tends to expand indefinitely. A gas is therefore in equilibrium only when it is completely enclosed. A liquid is relatively incompressible, and if all pressure, except that of its own vapor pressure, is removed, the cohesion between molecules holds them together, so that the liquid does not expand indefinitely. Therefore a liquid may have a free surface, i.e. a surface from which all pressure is removed, except that of its own vapor.

A *vapor* is a gas whose temperature and pressure are such that it is very near the liquid phase. Thus steam is considered a vapor because its state is normally not far from that of water. A gas may be defined as a highly superheated vapor, that is, its state is far removed from the liquid phase. Thus air is considered a gas because its state is normally very far from that of liquid air.

The volume of a gas or vapor is greatly affected by changes in pressure or temperature or both. It is usually necessary, therefore, to take account of changes in volume and temperature when dealing with gases or vapors. Whenever significant temperature or phase changes are involved in dealing with vapors and gases, the subject is largely dependent on heat phenomena (*thermodynamics*). Thus fluid mechanics and thermodynamics are interrelated.

Daugherty, Franzini & Finnemore. *Fluid Mechanics with Engineering Applications*, pp 1–2. McGraw-Hill, 1985.

G. Check your understanding

1. Complete these sentences using information from the text:

- The molecules of a fluid are _____ than those of a solid.
- The attractive forces between the molecules of a fluid are _____ as those of a solid.
- A liquid is much less _____ than a gas.
- If it is not completely enclosed, a gas will _____.
- The state of a vapour is not _____ the liquid phase.
- Changes in pressure and/or temperature _____ the volume of a gas or vapour.

2. Which words or phrases used in the text mean the following:

- to keep the same shape
- to get back its former shape
- to give back its former shape
- to change
- to stop

- to disappear
- to take away
- to get bigger (in volume)
- to be changed or influenced
- to take notice of or consider

3. Notice that the word 'tend' is used quite frequently: e.g. A solid *tends* to retain its shape.
- Can you explain what this means in your own words?
- Find three other sentences in the text where 'tend' is used.

4. How would you define:
- a viscous liquid?
- a vapour?

H. Understanding discourse

Listen to the conversation. Hamid is a student at a British University. It is his first term and he still finds many things rather strange — especially British plugs . . .

Now answer these questions:

1. What does Hamid need to know? Why?

2. Look at the diagram of the plug. Label the wires: *green*, *brown* and *blue* according to where they should go.

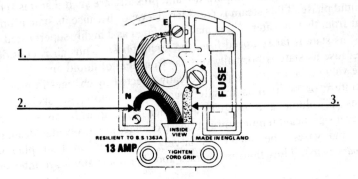

3. Now complete the instructions:

● Place the wire in the hole and _____ the screw.
● If the wire is too long, _____ it.
● After connecting the wires to the terminals, _____.
_____

● For a cassette player, use a _____ fuse.
● After screwing the cord grip down tight, _____
_____

● _____ the two parts of the casing together with a screw.

4. Practise explaining how to wire the plugs that you use in your country.

A. Understanding a printed text (1)

The following text introduces one kind of **air-conditioning system**. As you read, try to find the answers to the following questions. Remember, you do not have to understand all the words to answer the questions.

1. What are the functions of a thermal distribution system?

2. What are the six main elements of the air-conditioning system?
3. When is outdoor ventilation air needed?
4. A standard outdoor-air control plan must do two things. What are they?
5. What is one of the main aims of modern mixed-air temperature control systems?

Thermal distribution systems

In most medium-sized and large buildings, the thermal energy is transferred by means of air, water, and occasionally refrigerant. The transfer of energy often requires conveying energy from a space to a central heat sink (refrigeration unit) or conveying heat from a heat source (heater or boiler) to the space. The assembly that transfers heat between the conditioned spaces and the source or sink is called the thermal distribution system. Another of its functions is to introduce outdoor ventilation air.

We will now give an explanation of the classic single-zone system, which would be used for a large auditorium, for example, where precise conditions are to be maintained.

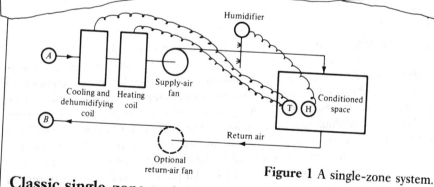

Figure 1 A single-zone system.

Classic single-zone system

The elements of the air-conditioning systems that will provide heating (and humidification) or cooling (and dehumidification) are shown in Figure 1. A subsystem of this interfaces with the facility shown in Figure 1 at points A and B. From point A the air flows to the cooling coil, heating coil, fan and humidifier toward the conditioned space. In the return-air line a fan is often installed to avoid excessive air pressure in the conditioned space relative to the outside air pressure. The temperature control is provided by a thermostat regulating the cooling or heating coil, and the humidity is controlled by a humidistat that regulates the humidifier.

Outdoor-air control

The introduction of outdoor ventilation air is necessary when the conditioning space is occupied by people. In many comfort air-conditioning installations the minimum percentage of outdoor ventilation air is between 10 and 20 per cent of the total flow rate of supply air. In some special applications, e.g. hospital operating rooms, the supply air may come exclusively from outdoors and be conditioned to maintain the specified space conditions. No return air is circulated in these installations.

The outdoor-air control mechanism that interfaces with the air system of Figure 1 and other air systems is shown in Figure 2. The stream of return air at B flowing back from the zones divides, some exhausting and some recirculating. The outdoor ventilation air mixes with the recirculated air and flows to the conditioning unit at A. Dampers in the outdoor-, exhaust-air lines open and close in unison and in the direction opposite the motion of the recirculated-air dampers.

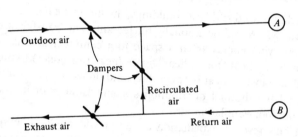

Figure 2 Outdoor-air control.

A standard outdoor-air control plan attempts to maintain the mixed-air temperature at point A at approximately 13° to 14°C since the basic function of the air-conditioning system is to provide cooling. Another requirement of the outdoor-air control is to assure that the minimum percentage of outdoor air is maintained. At a high outdoor temperature the dampers provide the minimum flow rate of outdoor air. At an outdoor temperature lower than about 24°C, it is more economical in cooling energy to use 100 per cent outdoor air. For outdoor-air temperatures below 13°C the dampers proportion themselves to maintain a mixed temperature of 13°C. To hold a mixed-air temperature of 13°C at extremely low outdoor temperatures, the fraction of outdoor air could drop below the minimum. The controls are therefore designed to hold to that minimum and allow the mixed-air temperature to drop below 13°C.

The traditional practice has been to try to achieve a mixed-air temperature year round of approximately 13°C, but current practice is influenced by the desire to conserve energy; so the mixed-air temperature may be reset to a higher value if and when cooling loads can be met by higher-temperature air.

F. Stoeker & J.W. Jones, *Refrigeration and Air Conditioning*, pp 89–92. McGraw-Hill, 1982.

B. Check your understanding

Now study the text carefully. As you do, look for answers to these questions:

1. How is thermal energy normally transferred in heating and cooling systems?

2. In an air-conditioning system, where does the air flow after it has passed through the cooling and heating coils?

3. What do we call the air that flows to the conditioned space?

4. What do we call the air that flows from the conditioned space?

5. What is the normal percentage of outdoor air used in air-conditioning installations?

6. What is the percentage of outdoor air supplied to hospital operating rooms?

7. In outdoor-air control mechanisms, what happens to the return air?

8. If an outdoor air control system is used, the supply air is a mixture. What two kinds of air does this mixture consist of?

9. What is the function of the dampers?

Now see if you can complete the graph below. Use the information given in paragraph 6.

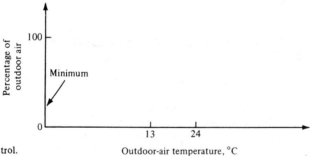

Outdoor-air control.

C. Increase your vocabulary

1. Find the words or phrases used in the text which express these ideas of *size and accuracy*:

- neither large nor small
- too high
- very low
- exact
- roughly/not exactly

2. The following verbs all describe movement. The underlined words are used in the text. Choose the correct word to complete each of the sentences below:

- transfer
- transport
- convey
- circulate
- recirculate
- flow

- Pipes _____ hot water from the boiler to every part of the building.
- Goods are _____ by truck from the port to their destination.
- In a closed refrigeration system, the fluid (e.g. water) _____ and _____.
- In some countries, the students can _____ from one university to another.
- In an air-conditioning system, the cool air _____ from the supply-air line to the conditioned space.

3. These words are used in the text to describe <u>control</u>.

- regulate • (re-)set • maintain
- conserve

Choose the correct verb to complete each of these sentences:

- Valves are used to _____ the flow-rate of the fluid.
- To alter the temperature of a heating or cooling system, we must _____ the thermostat.
- In an efficient air-conditioning system, the temperature indoors is _____ at a fixed level.

- Since natural sources of energy are in short supply, it is important to _____ energy as much as possible.

Can you find any other words or phrases in the text which also express <u>control</u>?

4. Can you explain the following words and phrases?

- comfort
- in unison
- assure
- traditional
- current

D. Check your grammar

1. EXPRESSING REASONS

Notice this sentence from the text:

A standard outdoor-air control plan attempts to maintain the mixed-air temperature at approximately 13° to 14°C *since* the basic function of the air-conditioning system is to provide cooling.

We could also say:

Because the function is to provide cooling, the temperature must be maintained at 13° to 14°C.
or
As the function is to provide cooling . . .

Notice the difference between *because* and *because of*:
He turned on the air conditioning *because* it was a hot day.
He turned on the air conditioning *because of* the heat.

Now express the following reasons:

Fact		Reason
On a hot day, a minimum of outdoor air is used in the supply-air mixture	....	warm outdoor air would raise the temperature of the supply air.
On cold days, a minimum of outdoor air is used in the supply-air mixture	....	cold outdoor air would lower the temperature of the supply air below 13°C.
When the temperature of the outdoor air is 13°C 100% outdoor air can be used in the supply	....	economy
Laboratory equipment must be used carefully	....	the cost of replacing it.

Refrigeration is an important field of study	....	it has many uses and applications.
It is very useful to be able to read easily in English	....	many textbooks and scientific papers are written in English.

2. EXPRESSING PURPOSE

Notice how purpose is expressed in this sentence from the text:

A fan is often installed *to avoid* excessive air pressure.

We can also say:

A fan is installed *in order to avoid* excessive air pressure.
Or:
A fan is installed *so that* excessive air pressure can be avoided.

Now complete the following sentences using one of these patterns:

- A humidifier is used . . .
- A thermostat is used . . .
- Dampers are used in the outdoor-air control mechanism . . .
- The outdoor-air control plan is necessary . . .
- The temperature of supply air may be set to a higher value . . .
- Air-conditioning is desirable in hot climates . . .
- Central heating systems are desirable in cold climates . . .
- Food must be refrigerated . . .
- Engines need lubricating oil . . .
- Car bodies must have several coats of paint . . .

E. Understanding a lecture

You will hear the first part of a lecture. As you listen, make notes and then try to answer the questions below.
  The extract has been divided into sections to enable you to understand it more easily.

1. • What is this lecture about?
   • According to the introduction which the lecturer gave, what were the main uses of refrigeration that he is going to talk about?
   • How many of these uses were described in the extract you heard?

2. • Why is the study of air-conditioning systems different from that of industrial refrigeration?
   • What is the name given to the study of processes which occur at very low temperatures?
   • Air conditioning is important for maintaining comfortable temperatures for people in hot climates. What are its other uses?
   • What two industries are mentioned where the control of the temperature-humidity and quality of air is important?
   • What can happen to electronic equipment if it is not kept in controlled conditions?
   • What happens to many kinds of food if it is not refrigerated?
   • What sort of temperatures are needed for storing frozen fruit and vegetables?

▼

3. Now listen to the lecture again, and complete the next two exercises.

(a) As you listen, write down the words used by the lecturer to:
- begin the lecture
- begin the section on air conditioning systems
- begin the section on refrigeration in industrial processes

(b) Complete the following sentences according to the information given in the lecture:

- The industrial gas industry deals with . . .
- Heat which is generated by large numbers of people, lights and electrical equipment can be . . .
- In the printing industry, the ink may fail to dry if . . .
- In areas where electronic equipment is kept, clean air is very important to . . .
- If food such as meat and fish is refrigerated, . . .

(c) What do you think?
- What do you think the speaker was going to talk about next after the extract you heard?
- What other food processes can you think of in which temperature plays an important part?
- What do you think the lecturer's conclusions are going to be?

F. Understanding a printed text (2)

Read the following passage and take notes on the text.

Chemical and process industries

The chemical and process industries include the manufacturers of chemicals, petroleum refiners, petrochemical plants, paper and pulp industries, etc. These industries require good engineering for their refrigeration since almost every installation is different and the cost of each installation is so high. Some important functions served by refrigeration in the chemical and process industries are (1) separation of gases, (2) condensation of gases, (3) solidification of one substance in a mixture to separate it from others, (4) maintenance of a low temperature of stored liquid so that the pressure will not be excessive, and (5) removal of heat of reaction.

A mixture of hydrocarbon gases can be separated into its constituents by cooling the mixture so that the substance with the high-temperature boiling point condenses and can be physically removed from the remaining gas. Sometimes in petrochemical plants hydrocarbons, such as propane, are used as the refrigerant. Propane is relatively low in cost compared with other refrigerants, and the plant is completely equipped to handle flammable substances. In other applications separate refrigeration units provide refrigeration for the process.

Special applications of refrigeration

Other uses of refrigeration and air-conditioning span sizes and capacities from small appliances to the large industrial scale.

Drinking fountains Small refrigeration units chill drinking water for storage and use as needed.

Dehumidifiers An appliance to dehumidify air in homes and buildings uses a refrigeration unit by first passing the air to be dehumidified through the cold evaporator coil of the system, where the air is both cooled and dehumidified. Then this cool air flows over the condenser and is discharged to the room.

Ice makers The production of ice may take place in domestic refrigerators, ice makers serving restaurants and motels, and large industrial ice makers serving food-processing and chemical plants.

Ice-skating rinks Skaters, hockey players, and curlers cannot rely upon the weather to provide the cold temperatures necessary to freeze the water in their ice rinks. Pipes carrying cold refrigerant or brine are therefore embedded in a fill of sand or sawdust, over which water is poured and frozen.

Construction Refrigeration is sometimes used to freeze soil to facilitate excavations. A further use of refrigeration is in cooling huge masses of concrete (the chemical reaction which occurs during hardening gives off heat, which must be removed so that it cannot cause expansion and stress the concrete). Concrete may be cooled by chilling the sand, gravel, water, and cement before mixing, and by embedding chilled-water pipes in the concrete.

Desalting of seawater One of the methods available for desalination of seawater is to freeze relatively salt-free ice from the seawater, separate the ice, and remelt it to redeem fresh water.

Conclusion

The refrigeration and air-conditioning industry is characterised by steady growth. It is a stable industry in which replacement markets join with new applications to contribute to its health.

The high cost of energy since the 1970s has been a significant factor in stimulating technical challenges for the individual engineer. Innovative approaches to improving efficiency which once were considered impractical now receive serious consideration and often prove to be economically justified. An example is the recovery of low temperature heat by elevating the temperature level of this energy with a heat pump (which is a refrigeration system). The days of designing the system of lowest first cost with little or no consideration of the operating cost now seem to be past.

W.F. Stoecker & J.J. Jones, *Refrigeration and Air Conditioning*, pp 7–12. McGraw-Hill, 1982.

G. Check your understanding

See if you can answer these questions by referring to the notes you have taken and not to the original text.

1. Why do the chemical and process industries require good engineering for their refrigeration?

2. Name two of the processes in which refrigeration is important.

3. How can a mixture of hydrocarbon gases be separated into its constituent parts?

4. Can you name a hydrocarbon which is sometimes used as a refrigerant?

5. Name two small appliances which use refrigeration or air-conditioning systems.

Can you explain:
- how refrigeration is used in construction?
- how it is used for desalting seawater?

H. Understanding discourse

Listen to the conversation. Peter, an engineering student, talks to his tutor, Mr Edwards.

Now answer the following questions:

1. How does Peter get Mr Edwards' attention? What does he say?
2. What question does he ask?
3. What question does Mr Edwards ask Peter?
4. What does Mr Edwards say about Peter's work?
5. What is the first thing Peter asks for advice on?
6. What advice does Mr Edwards give?
7. What does Peter want to be able to do in his future career?
8. Does Mr Edwards think that refrigeration engineering would offer him opportunities to do this?
9. What is the third thing that Peter asks about?
10. What advice does Mr Edwards give him?

DIESEL ENGINES

A. Understanding a printed text (1)

This text will describe the **cylinder head** in a diesel engine, and will give instructions on how to remove it.
Read the passage through and find the answers to these questions. Remember, you do not have to understand every word to answer the questions.

1. What does the cylinder head do?
2. What is it made of?
3. What are the parts of a cylinder head called?
4. What part of the engine can you see when the cylinder head is removed?

The Cylinder Head

The cylinder head is cast as one piece. It is the upper sealing surface of the combustion chamber. It may serve one, two, three, four or six cylinders. The valve guides, which guide the valve stem during the opening and closing of the valve, are pressed into the cylinder head. All cylinder heads are made of a special iron alloy casting containing carbon, silicon, and copper. This alloy mixture provides elasticity and good thermal conductivity, and has a low thermal expansion rate. The size of the cylinder head is not determined by the number of cylinders but rather by such factors as the overall cost of the engine, the cylinder block design, the number of main bearings, the expected thermal stress, and the anticipated cooling and sealing difficulties (of the cylinder head).

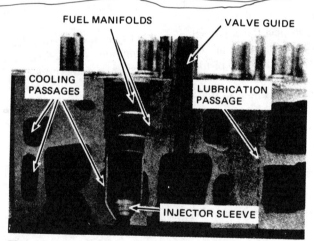

FUEL MANIFOLDS   VALVE GUIDE

COOLING PASSAGES

LUBRICATION PASSAGE

INJECTOR SLEEVE

Fig. 5-7 Sectional view of a cylinder head.

Whether an individual cylinder head is used for each cylinder (Fig. 5–7) or whether the cylinder head covers two, three, four or six cylinders, it must nevertheless have adequate strength and stiffness. It must act as a sealing surface between the cylinder sleeve, cylinder-block top deck, and oil and cooling passages, without distorting the sleeve or valves. The cylinder head must be sufficiently strong so that it does not crack between the cylinder-head bolts (studs), between the intake and exhaust valve, or between the valves and injector (sleeve or bore).

The internal cooling passages must be located to ensure that the coolant flow has a high velocity at and around the valves and injector tubes. It must remove heat (steam bubbles) and prevent the accumulation of deposit or scale. The passages should have no dead ends. The external openings must prevent turbulence and permit unrestricted circulation from the cylinder block to the cylinder head and from the cylinder head to the radiator.

The valves must be located so that the fuel spray can reach the total combustion area, but they must be far enough apart so that the coolant can circulate freely between them, thereby preventing the cylinder head from cracking between the valve seats.

Removal of Cylinder Head

Care should be taken when removing the cylinder-head bolts or nuts.

Caution Never remove the cylinder head when it is hot because it will become distorted (warped).

If the cylinder head is very heavy, use a hoist to lift it from the cylinder block. If it is small, screw the lift handles into the cylinder head to lift it from the block. If a cylinder head is excessively tight, do not drive a chisel or screwdriver between the cylinder block and head to remove it, as this will damage both surfaces. Lightly tap the cylinder head with a bronze or lead hammer or use a block of wood to break it loose.

Carefully inspect the combustion chamber once it is exposed. Close scrutiny can often reveal the cause of high oil consumption, overfueling, water leakage, or overheating. Damage to pistons, cylinder sleeves, and cylinder block can also be seen.

Caution When removing the cylinder head, take care not to damage it or the cylinder block surface or threads. If studs are used, take care not to bend them. After removal, place the cylinder head in a holding fixture, or if it happens to be square, you may place it on a workbench.

E.J. Schulz, *Diesel Mechanics* (second edition), pp 23–4. McGraw-Hill, 1983.

B. Check your understanding

Now study the text carefully. As you do, look for the answers to these questions:

1. The alloy used to make the cylinder head should have the following properties (tick all those which will complete the above sentence):

● strength	☐	● good electrical conductivity	☐
● flexibility	☐	● good thermal conductivity	☐
● ductility	☐	● stiffness	☐
● brittleness	☐	● low thermal expansion rate	☐
● elasticity	☐	● high thermal expansion rate	☐

2. The size of the cylinder head depends on (tick all the statements which are correct):

(a) the number of main bearings ☐
(b) the number of cylinders ☐
(c) the design of the cylinder block ☐
(d) the amount of thermal stress it must withstand ☐
(e) the cost of the engine ☐
(f) the cost of raw materials ☐

3. Tick all the statements below which refer to things that *must be done* or *must happen*:

(a) The coolant must flow quickly around the valves and injector tubes. ☐
(b) The fuel spray must reach the total combustion area. ☐
(c) The cooling passages must have dead ends. ☐
(d) Turbulence must be prevented. ☐
(e) The valves must be located as close together as possible. ☐
(f) The accumulation of scale must be prevented. ☐
(g) The cylinder head must be removed when it is hot. ☐
(h) A screwdriver must be used to loosen the cylinder head when removing it. ☐

4. What problems of a general kind might be discovered by removing the cylinder head and inspecting the combustion chamber?
Make a list (seven are mentioned in the text).

C. Increase your vocabulary

1. Notice the use of these words in the text:

- adequate/inadequate • sufficient • excessive

Read the following sentences and notice how they can be expressed in another way:

We had sufficient supplies to last three days.
= We had *enough* supplies to last three days.
The instructions they gave were inadequate.
= The instructions they gave were *not good enough*.
The costs were excessive (or: excessively high).
= The costs were *too high*.

Now re-write these sentences in the same way:

- The accumulation of deposit was excessive.
- The strength of the material was inadequate to withstand stress.
- The cylinder block cracked because it was not sufficiently strong.
- The mechanic used excessive force to remove the block.
- The inspection was not carried out with sufficient care.
- There is an inadequate amount of detail in the text.

2. Now look in the text to see how these words were used.

- provide • prevent • permit • ensure

When you have studied the use, decide which one can be used in each of these sentences:

- Lubricants are used to _____ friction.
- The coolant system must _____ the coolant to expand.
- An outlet is _____ so that excess coolant can escape.
- Piston rings must fit correctly to _____ proper sealing and oil control.

D. Check your grammar

1. POSSIBILITY AND CONDITION

> **Do you remember?**
> What will happen if . . .?
> > can
> > might
>
> Look at these examples:
>
> - *If* the bearings are not lubricated, they *will* become damaged.
> - *If* the seals fail, coolant *can* leak into the oil.
> - *If* the oil filter is not changed regularly, it *might* become blocked.

Now complete the following sentences with reference to the text:

- If the cylinder head is not sufficiently strong . . .
- If the coolant cannot flow freely between the valves . . .
- If the cylinder head is removed when it is hot . . .
- If a screwdriver is used to remove the cylinder head . . .
- If the engine is overheating . . .
- If scale accumulates in the cooling passages . . .

2. INSTRUCTIONS

Look at these different ways of expressing things you must do, and things you must not do:

What you must do:	What you must not do:
Be careful to clean tools. Remove the cylinder head. *Carefully* inspect the combustion chamber. Care *should be* taken when removing the bolts. *Make sure that* the coolant can flow freely.	Do not use a chisel. *Never* remove the cylinder head when hot. The bolts *should not be* tightened excessively *Make sure that* there are no dead ends.

Now express these instructions, using one of the forms given:

What you must do	*What you must not do:*
Keep work area clean and tidy.	Use cold water to flush the system when the engine is hot.
Change oil filters regularly. Examine bearings for wear. Use correct lubricants. Follow manufacturers' recommended instructions.	Spill acid on your skin. Smoke when checking batteries. Overcharge the batteries. Use a screwdriver as a scraper or chisel.

> Look at this example:
> If the cylinder head is heavy, use a hoist to lift it.

Now express these conditional instructions in the same way:

- Cylinder head is small   ....   use lift handles.
- Cylinder head is very tight   ....   tap it lightly with a hammer.
- Cylinder head is hot   ....   wait till it cools.
- Studs are used   ....   do not bend them.
- Cylinder head is square   ....   place on workbench after removing it.

E. Understanding a lecture

You will hear part of a lecture on lubrication.
1. As you listen, take notes and try to complete the table below:

Table to show the properties of various engine oils

Property	10W	20/20W	30	40	50
Specific gravity	31.7	29.1	28.8	27.5	27.4
Flash point (°C)		232.2	243.3	250.0	
Pour point (°C)		−26.1	−20.6	−17.8	
Viscosity index					

2. Now use your notes to answer these questions:

- What does the lecturer say is "one of the greatest enemies of the internal combustion engine"?
- What are the four main purposes of engine oil?
- How does engine oil reach the components which it protects?
- What are the most important properties of engine oil which are mentioned in the part of the lecture you have heard?

3. Now answer these questions about the lecture:

- When the lecturer introduces his lecture, what are the three main points he says he will cover?
- Which of these are described in the extract you heard?
- Did he finish describing the properties of engine oil, do you think?
- Which do you think is more interesting for the engineer studying diesel mechanics:
  (a) the viscosity of oils?
  (b) the pour point?

4. Write a short definition of each of the following:

Viscosity
The flash point
The pour point

F. Understanding a printed text (2)

Read the following passage:

Bearing Wear

Normal Bearing Wear Before you can diagnose abnormal wear, you must first understand what is considered to be normal wear. Most bearing wear that occurs during the first few hours of operation is minimal and accepted as 'normal'. The bearing shown in Fig. 17–7 was taken from a truck engine which was operated for 4500 hours. It shows normal wear. Under normal usage some of the thin lead-tin overlay surface wears off, exposing the lining (copper, nickel, or aluminum). The pattern of wear is concentrated toward the center of the bearing because of its larger diameter. When motortruck engine bearings show this wear within less than 2000 hours or 100,000 miles (mi) [160,930 km] of operation, the wear is considered to be abnormal, suggesting that abrasives have entered the oil. Check for the following: poor air filtration, intake manifold leakage, poor lubrication filtration, overfueling, or restricted engine breathing. Fine abrasives may also enter the oil during the engine rebuilding period or through carelessness while making oil and filter changes.

Most bearing failures are due to foreign matter (plain old dirt) passing between the journals and bearings. This also applies, of course, to other operating components. Depending on the type of foreign matter in the lubricant, the journals, bearings, and components may become scratched, pitted, or discolored, etc.

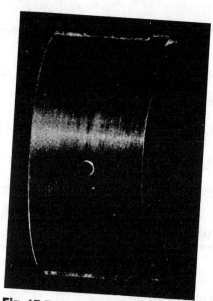

Fig. 17-7 Normal friction-bearing wear after long use. *[J.I. Case Agricultural Equipment Division (TENNECO).]*

How to Prevent Dirt From Contaminating Lubricant

1. To begin with, your work area and tools must be clean.
2. Before assembling the engine, make sure that all components and bores are clean. When the engine is not being worked on, cover it with plastic sheets to keep out any fine dust.
3. Keep all oil storage containers and measuring equipment clean.
4. Follow the manufacturer's recommended procedure when making oil and filter changes.
5. Avoid excessive delay between oil filter changes because this may cause the filter to become plugged.
6. When adding oil, wipe the area around the dipstick clean before reinserting.
7. Remember that the entry of even a small amount of dirt into the lubricant will create extensive damage at a later date.

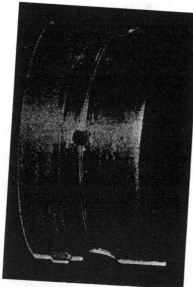

Fig. 17-8 Damage caused by coarse particles.   *(Cummins Engine Company, Inc.)*

Bearing Failure due to Coarse Particles in Oil

Coarse particles may originate as residue from moving engine components, from improper handling of lubricant or oil filters, or from incomplete removal of honing or boring abrasives.

The bearing shell shown in Fig. 17–8 will fail completely because of the long deep scratches which decrease the efficiency of the lubricant and heat dissipation. The visible particles have displaced metal (aluminum) and have added to the abrasion, causing heat to build up and melt the lead surface. However, if the bearings show fine scratches and the consequence of embedded particles, but nevertheless the bearing surface is smooth and reformed, it can be reused.

E.J. Schulz, *Diesel Mechanics* (second edition), pp 97–100. McGraw-Hill, 1983.

Note: Use your dictionary, and make sure you know the meaning of these words describing *damage* to bearings:

Noun	Verb	Adjective/participle
wear	wear/wear off	worn
scratch	scratch	scratched
pit	pit	pitted
discolouration	discolour	discoloured
abrasion	—	—
leak/leakage	leak	leaking

G. Check your understanding

1. Tick all the instructions which are correct according to the text:

(a) Understand what normal wear is. ☐
(b) If wear shows within 2000 hours, do nothing. ☐
(c) When working on the engine, cover it with plastic sheets. ☐
(d) Remember to keep all equipment and tools clean. ☐
(e) Change oil and filters according to manufacturers' instructions. ☐
(f) Do not change oil filter unless it becomes plugged. ☐
(g) Wipe the dipstick clean before removing it. ☐
(h) Do not reuse bearings which show fine scratches and still have a smooth surface. ☐

2. Complete these statements according to information given in the text:

● If an engine bearing shows wear within less than about 160,000 km . . .
● Abrasives entering the oil cause . . .
● Carelessness while working on the engine can cause . . .
● Most bearing failures are caused by . . .
● The bearings may become scratched, pitted or discoloured as a result of . . .
● If the bearing shell becomes deeply scratched . . .
● If particles displace the metal and add to the abrasion . . .
● If the bearings have fine scratches and the surface is still smooth . . .

3. The *negative forms* and *opposites* of these words appear in the text. Can you find them?

● increase   ● coarse
● complete   ● careful
● proper   ● coloured
● clean   ● smooth
● normal

H. Understanding discourse

Listen to the conversation between two friends, Tom and Bill. Listen for the answers to the following questions:

1. What is the problem with Tom's car?
2. What question does Bill ask first, to try to find the cause of the trouble with Tom's car?

3. What are the possible reasons for the trouble?
4. Which of these possible reasons can be eliminated, according to what Tom says?
5. What other possible causes remain to be checked?
6. How can Tom check the electrical system?

DATA COMMUNICATIONS

UNIT 9

A. Understanding a printed text (1)

This text gives a brief history of the development of **data communications** and computer systems. As you read, look for the answers to these questions. Remember, you do not need to understand all the words to answer the questions.

1. Who invented the first mechanical device that could store numbers?
2. What were the problems of the first electronic computers?
3. What was the event that marked the start of the modern computer age?
4. What capability is essential in modern data communications?

14–2 Fundamentals of Data Communications Systems

Data communications became important when the rapid transfer of data became both necessary and feasible. In other words, data communications emerged as a natural result of the development of sophisticated computer systems. The milestones in this development are now outlined.

14–2.1 The Emergence of Data Communications Systems

Computer systems history The early history of the development of computing machines is replete with impressive names. The French scientist Blaise Pascal is credited with the invention of the first adding machine in 1642. His machine was mechanical in nature, using gears to store numbers.

The mechanical model was followed up in 1822 by Charles Babbage, professor of mathematics at Cambridge University in England. Babbage used gears and punched cards to produce the first general purpose digital computer, which he called the analytic engine, but it was never completed or put into use.

Census taking provided the incentive for Herman Hollerith to use punched cards in the first data processing operation. Their successful application to the 1890 U.S. National Census demonstrated the value to be realized from automatic data processing systems. The laborious, time-consuming task of sorting census data by hand was reduced in both time required and effort expended, because punched cards were put into the machine which automatically sorted them.

Howard Aiken of Harvard University combined the mechanical processes of Babbage with the punched-card techniques of Hollerith to develop an electromechanical computer. The Harvard Mark I, as it was called, was capable of multiplying and dividing at rates significantly faster than previously possible. The electromechanical nature of the device, which used punched cards and punched tape for data and control, limited its speed and capability, however.

The first fully electronic computer was developed at the University of Pennsylvania by Dr. John Mauchly and J. Presper Eckert, Jr. The computer used 18,000 electron tubes to make and store its calculations. Called the Electronic Numerical Integrator and Calculator (ENIAC), this device could, in 1946, multiply 300 numbers per second (approximately 1000 times as fast as Aiken's computer). As fast as ENIAC was, however, the lack of external control and the bulk and power consumption resulting from the use of vacuum tubes precluded large-scale production.

The milestone which marked the beginning of the modern age of computers was the development of the transistor. This device was significantly smaller than the electron tube, required much less electrical power to operate, and generated very much less heat. With the subsequent development of integrated circuits, it became possible to design equipment consisting of hundreds and thousands of transistors but requiring minimal space. This advance has made computers with amazing speed and impressive capability commonplace. Concurrently with the development of smaller, faster, and more sophisticated computers, developments in storage devices were also made.

Computer systems have been classed into three generations. The first generation consisted of vacuum-tube-based machines. They used magnetic drums for internal storage and magnetic tape for external storage. These computers were slow compared to modern machines and, owing to their bulk, they required data to be brought to them.

Second-generation computers using transistors began to appear in 1959. The internal storage used magnetic cores, with small doughnuts of magnetic material wired into frames that were stacked into large cores. This form of storage represented a tremendous increase in speed and reduction in bulk over previous storage methods. The external storage in second-generation computers used magnetic disks. This form of storage also added to increased speed and greater 'online' capability as compared to magnetic tape systems.

Beginning in 1964, a third generation of computers began to emerge. These computers utilized integrated circuits to increase capability and decrease size, while integrated technology also provided improved internal storage capability. Solid-state memory, being now totally electronic, greatly increased the speed and capacity of the internal memory while decreasing its cost and complexity. External memory continued to use magnetic disks, which became larger and faster.

It was stated that early computers required data to be brought to them. This data was usually prepared by using punch cards or magnetic tape. The cards or tapes would then be carried to the computer where they would be processed. The transfer of data in this fashion was called batch processing. Transport might be no farther than from the next room, or again, it might be from the other side of the world. As each batch of data was received, it was placed into line with other batches of data which were processed one after another. Reports were generated, files were updated, new tapes were made and the revised data was routed to appropriate locations in the form of punched cards or magnetic tape. The inefficiency of such a system is easily seen in retrospect.

Later-model computers are provided with the capability of handling numerous input devices directly. These multitask computers treat the incoming data in much the same way as the earlier computers did. Incoming data is received from the various input devices and is lined up, or queued by the computer. The computer will then process the incoming data according to internal procedures. If the computer reaches a place with one batch of data where it can link the data to storage, printers or other devices, the computer will begin to process another batch. The modern computers are so fast in their operation that they can handle many users without the users even being aware than others are on the system. This capability has made it necessary for computer data to be transported in ways other than by punch cards or magnetic tape. The ability of the computer to service many input-output devices simultaneously has made data communications essential.

G. Kennedy. *Electronic Communication Systems*, pp 489–490. McGraw-Hill, 1985.

B. Check your understanding

Now read the text more carefully. While you read, look for the answers to the following questions.

1. Complete the table below with information from the text about the early development of computer systems:

Name of inventor/ organisation	Date	Type/name of machine	Basis of operation
Blaise Pascal	1642	Adding machine	Mechanical: gears used to store numbers,
	1822		
Herman Hollerith		Automatic data processing system	
Howard Aiken Harvard University	—		
		ENIAC	

2. Match the characteristics of each generation of computers (given on the right-hand side) with the sequence on the left:

- A. First Generation
- B. Second Generation
- C. Third Generation

a. Used transistors. Data stored internally on magnetic disks.

b. Used integrated circuits, electronic solid-state memory. External memory stored on magnetic disks.

c. Vacuum-tube based machines. Magnetic drums used for internal storage and magnetic tape for external storage.

3. *Differences between early computers and later models.*

Fill in the missing details:

Early Computers	Later model computers
• Data needed to be brought to the computer	....
•	Can receive data from many kinds of input devices.
•	Data stored electronically.
•	Incoming data lined up and processed according to internal procedures.
• Users had to wait for 'time' on the computer.	....
• Only one source of input could be serviced at one time.	....

C. Increase your vocabulary

Remember, you can use your dictionary to help you answer these questions.

1. Find six words in the text which describe what computing machines can *do*.

2. Notice the words used to describe the different generations of computer.
Now complete the table below with appropriate adjectives or nouns. You can find most of them in the text.

Characteristic	Early models	Modern computers
• Speed		
•	Large	Small
• Time		Time-saving
• Effort		Easy/effortless
• Storage capacity		Unlimited
• Cost		
•		Efficient

3. Notice the use of these words in the text:

● invent   ● develop   ● emerge   ● demonstrate

Now write the appropriate word into each of the following sentences:

● The first steam engine was _____ by James Watt.

● Computers have now been _____ which respond to speech.

● Isaac Newton _____ the laws of gravity.

● With the development of integrated circuits, a new generation of microprocessors _____.

D. Check your grammar

1. PAST AND PRESENT PERFECT TENSES

> Notice these examples from the text:
>
> *Past:*
>
> ● The first electronic computer *used* electron tubes to make and store its calculations.
>
> ● In 1964, a third generation of computers *began* to emerge.
>
> Notice that both these sentences refer to a past event which is now finished and complete.
>
> *Present perfect:*
>
> ● This advance *has made* computers with amazing speed and impressive capability commonplace.
>
> ● The ability of the computer to service many input-output devices simultaneously *has made* data communications essential.
>
> Notice that these sentences refer to developments which affect the *present* situation. In other words these are not finished or completed events.

Now write the verbs in the following sentences in the *past* or *present perfect* tense according to the meaning:

● Charles Babbage _____ (produce) the first general purpose digital computer.

● Babbage's computer, unfortunately, _____ (never, use).

● Modifications to telephone circuits _____ (make) it possible to use the telephone system for transmitting electronic data.

● The low cost of producing silicon chips _____ (bring) electronic technology into our everyday life.

● Since the 1950s, the size of computers _____ (decrease) considerably.

● The first telecommunications satellite _____ (launch) in 1965.

● Since then, satellite communications _____ (become) essential to many fields of technology.

● A computer _____ (not yet, develop) which can create a work of art.

▼

2. RELATIVE PRONOUNS (1)

> Note these two examples:
>
> - Babbage produced the first general purpose digital computer, *which he* called the analytic engine.
> - The milestone *which* marked the beginning of the modern age was the development of the transistor.
>
> Notice that in the first example, the words *which he* can be omitted from the sentence without changing the meaning. But in the second example, the word *which* cannot be omitted.

Read the sentences below and tick all those in which the underlined phrases *can* be omitted:

(a) Giant valve computers, such as the one <u>which is</u> shown in the picture, required a lot of maintenance. ☐
(b) A central processor contains many cells, <u>which</u> at any time can be in one of two states: positively charged or negatively charged. ☐
(c) The punched card, <u>which was</u> devised by Hollerith in the 1880s, was a major step in the development of the computer. ☐
(d) A disk is a storage device <u>which</u> allows the computer system to store and retrieve data. ☐
(e) An information-retrieval system, <u>which is</u> called Dendral, was developed for organic chemists at Stanford University. ☐
(f) A computer memory may have, for example, 1,000 locations at <u>which</u> characters of information may be stored. ☐

3. RELATIVE PRONOUNS (2)

> When using relative pronouns (which, that etc.), be careful not to include an extra pronoun which is not needed.
>   This sentence is not correct in English:
>
> - A computer system consists of a Central Processing Unit and a number of devices, which *they* feed information to the Central Processing Unit and receive information from it.
>
> The word *they* must be omitted so that the sentence is correct.

Now re-write the following so that they are correct:

- In a logic flowchart there are rectangles which they indicate an action in a program.
- The most important shape in the flowchart is the diamond, which it indicates a decision.
- The diamond asks a question and then shows the actions which they may follow depending on whether the answer is yes or no.
- Parallelograms in the flowchart show an action which a peripheral device (e.g. a printer) is involved in it.
- A compiler is a name given to the software which it translates a program into machine code.
- The machine code is made up of binary digits which the central processor can deal with them.

E. Understanding a lecture

You will hear a lecture about the structure of computers. Listen for the answers to the following questions.

1. Complete the labels for the diagram below.

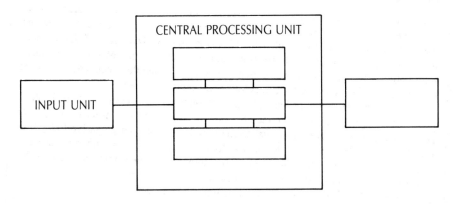

2. What are the functions of the three parts of the central processing unit?

Name | **Function**

● ....

● ....

● ....

3. Now match the terms on the left with the definitions on the right in the table below:

Term		**Definition**
● A.	A bit	(a) Binary patterns which are handled by the central processing unit.
● B.	A byte	(b) A piece of software that translates the programming language into machine code.
● C.	PASCAL	(c) A pattern of 8 bits representing data or instructions.
● D.	Machine code	(d) An example of a programming language.
● E.	A compiler	(e) A cell in the memory which can be positively or negatively charged.

▼

F. Understanding a printed text (2)

Read the following passage.

14-1 DIGITAL TECHNOLOGY

Digital technology is a branch of electronics and communications which utilizes *discontinuous signals*, i.e., signals which appear in discrete steps rather than having the continuous variations characteristic of analog signals. The value of digital techniques derives from the ability to construct unique codes to represent different items of information. These codes are the language of computers and the other types of digital electronic equipment which have revolutionized modern society.

Even though digital technology has been on the scene for only a relatively short period of time, it is difficult to remember how life was conducted prior to computers and their peripherals. Indeed, digital technology has become so pervasive today that few fields of endeavor remain for which digital processing is not important or even essential. Digital technology is of particular importance when information is to be gathered, stored, retrieved and/or evaluated. Digital processing is used so widely because it provides economical and rapid manipulation of data.

14-1.1 Digital Fundamentals

Comparison of analog and digital signals The meaning of the term "digital" is fundamental to an understanding of the benefits of digital technology. Digital data must be compared with analog data in order to understand the distinction between the two. An analog signal is best illustrated by a sine wave as shown in Fig. 14-1. Notice that the sine wave is continuous, and the value of the analog signal at any given instant can be anywhere within the range of the signal's extremes.

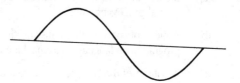

FIGURE 14-1   Sine wave; example of an analog signal.

The digital signal does not provide this continuous representation of the original signal. Instead, the digital signal represents data as a series of digits such as a number. This digital representation can be considered as a code which approximates the actual value. Various digital systems are available. For example, a digital system which is decimal in nature can be used to represent the sine wave. To do this, the range of values would be divided into 10 levels. The signal would then be sampled at set intervals and the appropriate level at that instant would be determined. Since only 10 levels would be available, however, the level which is closest would be used for a given sample if the signal were not to fall exactly on one of the levels. As shown in Fig. 14-2, the code could later be used to reconstruct the signal, producing a waveform similar to the original, with only minor discrepancies.

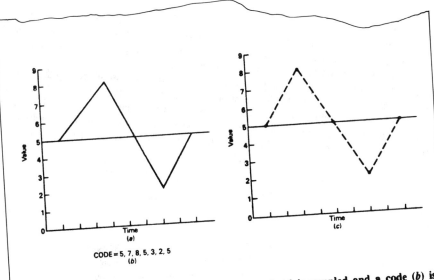

CODE = 5, 7, 8, 5, 3, 2, 5
(b)

FIGURE 14-2 Ten-level digitalization. (a) Analog signal is sampled and a code (b) is derived; (c) code is used to reconstruct original waveform.

The binary digital system The binary digital system is based on the binary numbering system. This system has only two numbers, 0 and 1. If the sine wave is represented by the most basic binary digital system, a 1 will be generated if the signal value is above the halfway point. A 0 will result from signals below the halfway point. Figure 14-3 shows the binary representation of the sine-wave signal. A series of the sine-wave cycles would generate a series of pulses with spaces between them as shown.

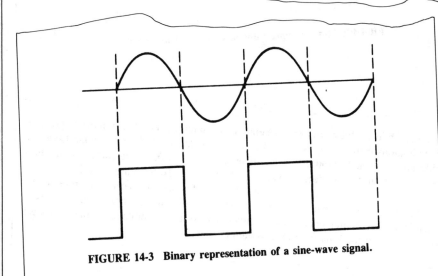

FIGURE 14-3 Binary representation of a sine-wave signal.

The word "digital," as it is commonly used in information systems, refers to information coded in the form of binary states. In the preceding chapter, it was shown that a binary code consists of a series of binary digits (or "bits") each of which can have either of only two values, either a 1 or a 0. When bits are assembled together into a group of a particular length, they form a binary word, sometimes called a byte. A single binary character can represent only two pieces of information, 0 or 1. As bits are assembled into words several bits in length, however, the number of code combinations increases. A binary word 2 bits in length can have four different forms, 00, 01, 10

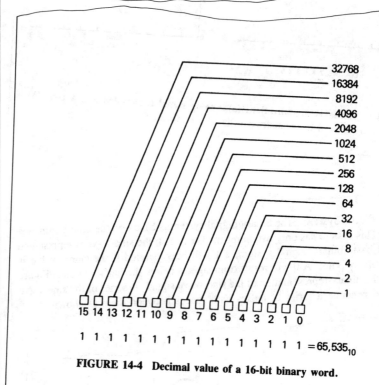

	32768
	16384
	8192
	4096
	2048
	1024
	512
	256
	128
	64
	32
	16
	8
	4
	2
	1

15 14 13 12 11 10 9 8 7 6 5 4 3 2 1 0

$$1\ 1\ 1\ 1\ 1\ 1\ 1\ 1\ 1\ 1\ 1\ 1\ 1\ 1\ 1\ 1 = 65{,}535_{10}$$

FIGURE 14-4 Decimal value of a 16-bit binary word.

and 11, while a 3-bit word can have eight code combinations. The number of possible combinations increases by powers of 2, so that binary words 8 bits in length have 256 different forms and 16-bit binary words provide over 65,000 code combinations. Figure 14-4 illustrates the decimal value of the bits in a 16-bit binary word.

If information is reduced to a standard set of codes which can be represented by binary words, the information can be handled by digital electronic devices. This is what is done in computers and digital processing systems. Digital computer codes are often based on the binary number system.

Kennedy. *Electronic Communication Systems*, pp 491–494. McGraw-Hill, 1985.

G. Check your understanding

1. Answer these general questions about the text:

- What kind of signals does digital technology make use of?
- Why is digital technology so widely used today?
- What two kinds of digital systems are described in the text?
- What are computer codes often based on?

2. Tick all the statements which are correct according to the text:

(a) Analog signals are continuous. ☐

(b) Digital electronic equipment requires the use of codes. ☐

(c) All digital systems are based on the binary numbering system. ☐

(d) A continuous waveform can be represented by code, and can be reconstructed to produce an exact duplication of the original. ☐

(e) A continuous wave represented by the binary system is received as a series of pulses. ☐

(f) A binary word 6 bits in length has 128 different combinations. ☐

H. Understanding discourse

Listen to the discussion about computers. Then answer the questions:

1. What question are the two people discussing?

2. Make a list of things which computers can do.

3. Now make a list of things which they can't do.

4. Will there ever be a computer that has feelings?
   (a) What opinion is expressed on the tape?
   (b) What is your opinion?

ELECTRIC POWER SYSTEMS

A. Understanding a printed text (1)

This text will provide you with some facts about devices which are used to protect **electric systems**. Pay attention to the way it is organised into paragraphs and sections. Notes in the margins will help you to refer to details quickly if necessary.

Now look at these questions and read the passage through to find the answers. Remember, you do not have to understand every word in order to do so.

1. Are all disturbances in normal operation caused by equipment failure?
2. How many different zone classifications are mentioned?
3. Do electromechanical relays operate slowly or quickly?
4. What overcurrent protection device is used in homes?
5. What devices are used to handle problems associated with interruption of large fault currents?

Electric Protection Devices

Causes of abnormal conditions in electric power systems

1 This term refers to a particular type of equipment applied to electric power systems to detect abnormal conditions and to initiate appropriate action to correct the abnormal condition. From time to time, disturbances in the normal operation of electric power systems occur. These may be caused by natural phenomena, such as lightning, wind, or snow; by accidental means traceable to reckless drivers, inadvertent acts by plant maintenance personnel, or other acts of human beings; or by conditions produced in the system itself, such as switching surges, load swings, or equipment failure.

2 Protective devices must therefore be installed on a power system to ensure continuity of electric service, to prevent injury to personnel, and to limit damage to equipment when abnormal situations develop. Application of these devices varies widely since they are applied commensurately with the degree of protection required.

The principle of zone protection

3 Zone Protection. For the purpose of applying protection, power systems are divided into areas, or zones. Each component of a power system falls into one of five different zone classifications: generator, transformer, bus, transmission line, or motor. Protection devices are applied to each zone to detect abnormal system conditions within that zone and to initiate actions for the removal of that zone from the rest of the system. Figure 1 illustrates the principle of zone protection on a simple power system. Note that complete protection is afforded by overlapping zones. Removal of only the malfunctioning part of the system ensures maximum electric service continuity.

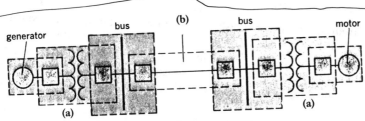

Fig. 1. Zones of protection on simple power system.

4 Protective Relays. These are used to sense changes in the voltages and currents on a power system. Sufficiently large variations from normal in these quantities can cause the relay to operate. Operation of the relay results in opening of circuit breakers to isolate that portion of the power system experiencing an abnormal voltage or current condition. A fault in one part of the system affects all other parts of the system. Therefore, relays throughout the power system must be coordinated to ensure the best quality of service to the loads, and to isolate equipment near the fault to prevent excessive damage or personal hazard.

The function of protective relays

5 Electromechanical relays are built to respond to voltage, current, or a combination of both. Operation of the relay either opens or closes a contact. Two basic principles are used in the making of electromechanical relays. The simplest type of relay operates on the electromagnetic attraction principle. This relay is composed of a coil, plunger and set of contacts, as shown in Figure 2. When current (I) flows in the coil, a force is produced that causes the plunger to move and close the relay contacts. These relays are characterized by their fast operating time.

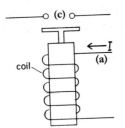

Fig. 2. Plunger relay.

The construction and operation of electromagnetic relays

6 The electromagnetic induction principle is also used as a basic building block in the construction of induction relays. This type of relay responds to alternating current only, whereas the relays discussed above respond to either direct or alternating current. Briefly, an induction relay consists of an electromagnetic circuit, a disk or other form of rotor made of nonmagnetic current-carrying material, and contacts. A schematic illustration of an induction-type relay is shown in Figure 3. By use of the principles of electromagnetic attraction and electromagnetic induction, protecting relays can be built to respond to all abnormal conditions that may occur in practice.

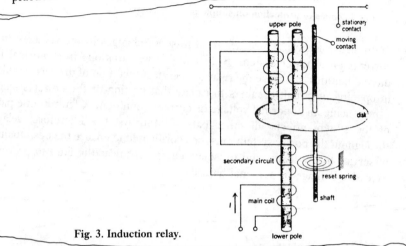

Fig. 3. Induction relay.

7   Overcurrent Protection. This must be provided on all systems to prevent abnormally high currents from overheating and causing mechanical stress on equipment. Overcurrent in a power system usually indicates that current is being diverted from its normal path by a short circuit. In low-voltage, distribution-type circuits, such as those found in homes, adequate overcurrent production can be provided by fuses that melt when current exceeds a predetermined value. Small, thermal-type circuit breakers also provide overcurrent protection for this class of circuit.

8   As the size of circuits and systems increases, the problems associated with interruption of large fault currents dictate the use of power circuit breakers. Normally, these breakers are not equipped with elements to sense fault conditions, and therefore overcurrent relays are applied to measure the current continuously. When the current has reached a predetermined value, the relay contacts close. This actuates the trip circuit of a particular breaker, causing it to open and thus isolate the fault.

Encyclopedia of Science and Technology, pp 496–501. McGraw-Hill, 1970.

Domestic and industrial overcurrent protection devices

B. Check your understanding

Answer these questions. Remember to use your dictionary if necessary.

1. Supply appropriate examples to complete these lists which show causes of disturbances to electric power systems.

Natural	Human	Equipment
....	....	....
....	....	....
....	....	....

- Write down the three purposes served by protection devices.
- Supply the missing words indicated by (a) and (b) in Fig. 1.
- What is the purpose of overlapping zones in zone protection?
- What causes protective relays to operate?
- Supply the missing words indicated by (a), (b) and (c) in Fig. 2.
- To what types of current does a plunger relay respond?
- What effect can overcurrent have on equipment?
- What protective device, besides fuses, is used in homes?
- Why do systems with power circuit breakers also need overcurrent relays?

2. Are the statements below True (T) or False (F)?

- The type of electric protection device used varies according to their need. ☐
- Zone is another word for area. ☐
- Protective relays repair faults in electric systems. ☐
- Plunger and induction relays are exactly the same. ☐
- Power circuit breakers open when relay contacts close. ☐

3. *Explanations*

- Can you explain what is meant by: 'Disturbances may be caused by accidental means traceable to careless drivers?'?
- Complete this sentence:
  Protective relays operate when . . .
- Describe briefly, in your own words if possible, how plunger relays operate.

C. Increase your vocabulary

You will need to use your dictionary in these exercises.

1. Difficult plural forms. The word 'phenomena' in paragraph 1 is the plural of the word 'phenomenon'. Before using a dictionary, can you think of the singular form of these words?

- criteria
- axes
- data
- crises
- appendices
- indices
- matrices
- vortices

- Is there anything unusual about 'indices', 'matrices' and 'vortices'?

2. Find words, in the paragraphs indicated, which can have similar meanings to those listed below.
- to find (paragraph 1)
- to set into operation (paragraph 1)
- in proportion to (2)
- amount (2)
- provided by (3)
- to separate (4)
- danger (4)
- consists of (5)
- to react to (6)
- being turned away from (7)

3. What is the difference between the following pairs of words which can sound similar?

- personnel (paragraph 1)/personal (paragraph 4)
- principle (paragraph 3)/principal
- to initiate (paragraph 1)/to initial
- to isolate (paragraph 4)/to insulate
- to affect/an effect

▼

4. *Verb plus preposition.* In engineering and technical texts, there are many verbs which must be followed by a particular preposition to express the correct meaning.

Example: These relays are *characterised* by their fast operating time.

Put *of/by/to/with* after the verbs below.

- to consist _____
- to respond _____
- to be composed _____
- to deal _____

- to apply _____
- to be caused _____
- to be associated _____
- to belong _____

D. Check your grammar

1. PREFIXES AND SUFFIXES

When reading texts you will often see many unfamiliar words. It is often possible to guess the meaning of these words if you understand the way words in English can be formed.

---

prefix + stem + suffix

Prefixes usually change the MEANING of the word.
Suffixes change the word from one PART OF SPEECH to another.

Examples: *unfamiliar:* 'un-' means not. Not familiar.
　　　　　 to simplify: '-ify' changes simple to the verb.

Prefixes. Notice how these prefixes change the meaning.
　　　*mal*functioning: not functioning correctly
　　　*over*heating: becoming too hot
　　　*pre*determined: decided in advance

(a) Look through the text again. How many words with prefixes can you find and what is their meaning?

(b) Rewrite the sentences below using words with prefixes. Do not change the meaning of the sentence. Choose from the prefixes you are given.

Example: The wheels are *not aligned correctly.*
　　　　　 The wheels are *misaligned.*

Prefixes: un-/mono-/mis-/re-/de-/

- The conditions were not satisfactory so the test was stopped.
- The cycle was not usual because it had only one wheel.
- Your notes are not clear so organise them again.
- Write this again because the style is not scientific.
- This coil has lost its magnetic properties.

(c) **Suffixes.** Rewrite these sentences using words with suffixes.

Example: He *made* the exercise *more simple to do.*
　　　　　 He *simplified* the exercise.

Suffixes: -ify/-less/-ly/-ise/-ible/-ive

- It is not difficult to make a piece of metal into a magnet.
- This design was produced without much care.
- He was able to tell me the identity of the part.
- It is possible to bend or flex many plastic materials.
- He did not communicate his ideas very well.

It is possible to express ideas using noun structures or verb structures. The latter are often used when speaking and the former are often used when writing.

Look at this example:
Application of these devices varies greatly.
These devices can be applied in many different ways.

Rewrite the sentences below using verb structures.

● Removal of the faulty part from the system ensures maximum electric service continuity.
● Interference with any part of the system causes an alarm to ring loudly.
● Activation of the safety relief valve results in a controlled reduction of pressure.

E. Understanding a lecture

You will now hear part of a lecture about electric power transmission. As you listen, you will have to answer questions and complete a graph. There will be a pause after each section of the lecture to allow you to complete the tasks.

Section 1

(a) What two factors are important in the transmission of power?

(b) Look at the incomplete graph.
● Write down the years 1890 to 1970 on the graph according to the information given.
● Write down the numbers 100 to 900 following the lecturer's words.
● What do the numbers in the vertical axis represent?

Section 2

Completing the graph.

(a) Draw the graph which the lecturer is explaining by placing dots (●) to indicate the maximum voltages transmitted in the years mentioned.

(b) Connect the dots on the graph with solid lines to show the increase in maximum transmission voltage from 1890 to 1970.

Section 3

● Are there any direct-current transmission systems in operation at the time the lecturer is talking about?
● What is the main problem associated with direct-current transmission?

Growth of Power Transmission

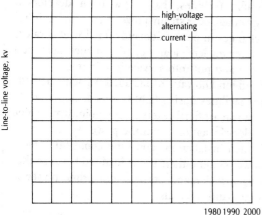

1980 1990 2000

Year

▼

F. Understanding a printed text (2)

Read the text below. Notice that it does not have a title or section headings. You will be required to provide them.

(a).................·

A little over 80% of the electric power used in the United States is obtained from generators driven by steam turbines. The largest turbine in service at this time (1968) is rated 1,130.000 killowatts (kw), equivalent to about 1,500,000 horsepower (hp). However, much larger units of over 1 million kilowatts are under construction.

(b).................·

(c)............. Coal is the fuel for more than half of the steam-turbine generation. Natural gas is used extensively in the south United States and heavy fuel oil is burned in a number of power plants where they can take delivery from ocean-going tankers.

(d)............. Despite the rapid development of nuclear power plants, uranium is the energy source for only about 2 or 3% of the steam-turbine generation in the United States. As the many nuclear plants under construction or planned go into commercial operation, however, they will cause a sharp rise in the percentage of steam-turbine generation fueled by uranium.

(e)............. Waterpower is still an important energy source in the United States, although in 1970 it supplied only about 17% of the electric power consumed. This is because most of the best sites, where sufficient water drops far enough to drive reasonable-sized hydraulic turbines, have now been developed. Waterpower offers one distinct advantage over steam-power plants in that it has greater flexibility in adapting to changes in power demands. Hydro-generators can even be shut down to store water for later loan periods; in such operation the idle generators can be restarted and put into service in minutes.

Some plants, totalling several million kilowatts of installed capacity, actually draw power from other generating facilities during light system-loan periods to pump water from a river or lake into an artificial reservoir at a point from which it can be drawn through a hydroelectric station when the power system needs additional generation. Although such installations consume about 50% more energy than they return to the power system, their use is justified because they can convert surplus power during low-demand periods into prime power to serve system needs during peak-demand intervals.

(f)----------------.

Generators of this type are used but only to provide a small amount of the total energy generated. Typical unit ratings for gas-turbine generators are 10,000–20,000 kw, but many plants have many such units to increase capacity. The average size of the diesel generator (about 2,000 kw per unit) is very small, but, like the gas-turbines, they offer extremely flexible operation, being capable of frequent start-ups. Therefore, they are very useful in emergencies or during load peaks.

(g)----------------.

(h)........... Power delivered by transmission circuits must be stepped down in facilities called substations to voltages more suitable for use in industrial and residential areas. On transmission systems, these facilities are commonly called bulk-power substations; on or near factories or mines, they are termed industrial substations; and where they supply residential and commercial areas, distribution substations. Basic equipment in a substation includes circuit breakers, switches, transformers and protective devices. There is also instrumentation, control devices and other apparatus related to specific function in the power system.

(i)........... That part of the electric power system that takes power from a bulk-power substation to customers' switches, commonly about 40% of the total plant investment, is called distribution. Primary distribution circuits usually operate at 4,160–34,500 volts line-to-line and may be overhead open wire on poles, overhead or aerial cable, or underground cable. These circuits supply large commercial, institutional and some industrial customers directly. Smaller customers are supplied through numerous distribution transformers. At conveniently located distribution transformers in residential and commercial areas, the voltage is stepped down again to 120 and 240 volts for secondary lines, from which service drops or loops extend to every customer's lights and appliances. These low voltages are known as utilization voltages.

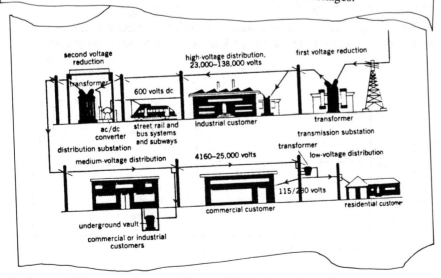

Distribution of Electricity, *Encyclopedia of Science and Technology*. McGraw-Hill, 1970.

G. Check your understanding

1. ● Select a title (a) for the text from the three below.
   Generation, Transmission and Distribution of Electric Power.
   Generation and Distribution of Electric Power.
   Sources of Generation of Electric Power.

● Write the letters (b) to (i) next to the appropriate section or paragraph heading to show its place in the text.
   … Hydro-electric.
   … Generating Power Sources.
   … Substations
   … Gas-turbine and Diesel Generators
   … Coal
   … Substations and Distribution
   … Nuclear
   … Distribution

● In 1968, what was the most common fuel used for steam-turbine generation of electricity?

● What factor affects the location of fuel-oil power stations?

● What was the maximum generating capacity of a nuclear power plant at this time?

● Why is it unlikely that more hydro-electric power plants will be developed?

● Give one advantage and one disadvantage of gas-turbine and diesel generators.

● What are substations used for?

● What size of circuit is used to supply large commercial customers?

● What is the typical voltage range in residences?

2. *Describing a process*
● Read the second paragraph on Waterpower again. In your own words, as much as possible, describe what happens in 'Some plants'.
   Now, write your description giving only the main facts about these plants.

Explaining
● Explain the phrases below in your own words.

   low-demand period
   idle generators
   capable of frequent start-ups
   light system-load periods

H. Understanding discourse

Listen to your tape again. You will hear someone describing the block diagram below. Listen for the words he uses to talk about changes in the information shown on the diagram.

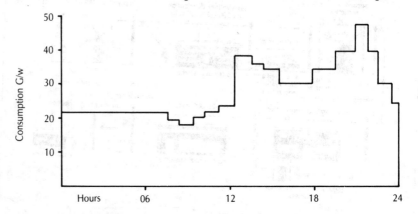

Daily Consumption of Electric Power in the UK

Listen to the description again. This time, write down next to the diagram below the words you have heard which can be used to express what they show about change.

1.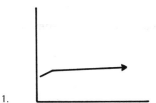

2.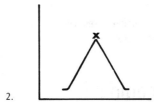

3.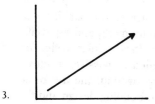

4.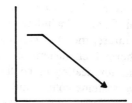

1. Consumption . . .
2. Consumption . . .
3. Consumption (a) . . .
            (b) . . .
            (c) . . .
4. Consumption (a) . . .
            (b) . . .
            (c) . . .

- What are the causes of the changes in consumption of electricity as shown on the diagram?

▼

The following exercises will help you to check how well you are continuing to learn the skills needed for study.

A. Reading

Read the text below and answer the questions on it.

Solar Energy Systems

The basic purpose of any solar energy system is to collect solar radiation and convert it into useful thermal energy. System performance depends on several factors, including availability of solar energy, the ambient air temperature, the characteristics of the energy requirement, and especially the thermal characteristics of the solar system itself. Solar collection 5 systems for heating or cooling are usually classified as passive or active. Passive systems collect and distribute solar energy without the use of an auxiliary energy source. They are dependent upon building design and the thermal characteristics of the materials used.

Active systems, on the other hand, consist of components which are to a 10 large extent independent of the building design and often require an auxiliary energy source for transporting the solar energy collected to its point of use. Active systems are more easily applied to existing buildings.

The major components of an active system are shown in Fig. 20–7. First the collector intercepts the sun's energy. A part of this energy is lost as it is 15 absorbed by the cover glass or reflected back into the sky. Of the remainder absorbed by the collector, a small portion is lost by convection and reradiation, but most is useful thermal energy, which is then transferred via pipes or ducts to a storage mass or directly to the load as required. Energy storage is usually necessary since the need for energy may not coincide with 20 the time when solar energy is available. Thermal energy is distributed either directly after collection or from storage to the point of use. The sequence of operation is managed by automatic and/or manual system controls.

Several types of solar collectors are available, and selection of one or another will depend on the intended application. Collectors are classified as 25 fixed or tracking. The tracking collectors are controlled to follow the sun throughout the day. Such systems are rather complicated and generally only used for special high-temperature applications. Fixed collectors are much simpler. Although their position or orientation may be adjusted on a seasonal basis, they remain 'fixed' over a day's time. Fixed collectors are less 30 efficient than tracking collectors; nevertheless they are generally preferred as they are less costly to buy and maintain.

Collectors may also be classified as flat-plate or concentrating. Concentrating collectors use mirrored surfaces or lenses to focus the collected solar energy on smaller areas to obtain higher working temperatures. Flat- **35** plate collectors may be used for water heating and most space-heating applications. High-performance flat-plate or concentrating collectors are generally required for cooling applications since higher temperatures are needed to drive absorption-type cooling units.

The flat-plate collector consists of an absorber plate, cover glass, **40** insulation, and housing. The absorber plate is usually made of copper and coated to increase the absorption of solar radiation. The cover glass (or glasses) are used to reduce convection and reradiation losses from the absorber. The housing holds the absorber (insulated on the back and edges) and cover plates. The working fluid (water, ethylene glycol, air, etc.) is **45** circulated in a serpentine fashion through the absorber plate to carry the solar energy to its point of use. The temperature of the working fluid in a flat-plate collector may range from 30 to 90°C, depending on the type of collector and the application. The collection efficiency of flat-plate collectors varies with design, orientation, time of day, and the temperature **50** of the working fluid. The amount of solar irradiation reaching the top of the outside glazing will depend on the location, orientation, and tilt of the collector. The amount of useful energy collected will also depend on the optical properties (transmissivity and reflectivity), the properties of the absorber plate (absorptivity and emissivity), and losses by conduction, **55** convection, and reradiation.

Answer these questions.

1. The most important factor in solar energy system performance is

- the availability of solar energy. ☐
- the ambient air temperature. ☐
- the type of energy required. ☐
- the thermal characteristics of the system. ☐

2. Active solar collection systems

- do not need an additional energy source. ☐
- need an additional energy source. ☐
- are only used for heating. ☐
- are only used for cooling. ☐

▼

3. The solar collector

- absorbs all of the sun's energy. ☐
- reflects all of the sun's energy. ☐
- absorbs some of the sun's energy. ☐
- absorbs none of the sun's energy. ☐

4. Another way of expressing 'to a large extent' is (line 9/10)

- mostly ☐
- totally ☐
- slightly ☐
- frequently ☐

5. The word 'major' (line 13) here means

- biggest ☐
- main ☐
- largest ☐
- best ☐

6. Fixed solar collectors are used more than tracking collectors

- because they are simpler in design. ☐
- because they are cheaper to buy and maintain. ☐
- because they can produce high temperatures. ☐
- because they stay in one position all day. ☐

7. Is the statement below correct according to the text?

Concentrating collectors concentrate the sun's energy so that a smaller area can be heated.
- correct ☐
- incorrect ☐

8. Which of these statements is correct?

(a) The cover glass on flat-plate collectors decreases the amount of heat absorbed by the collector. ☐
(b) The cover glass on flat-plate collectors increases the amount of heat absorbed by the collector. ☐

9. Is the statement below correct or incorrect?

The position of fixed solar collectors can never be changed.
- correct ☐
- incorrect ☐

10. The amount of energy a flat-plate collector can gather

- depends on its design. ☐
- depends on several factors. ☐
- depends on the temperature. ☐
- depends on the time of day. ☐

B. Writing

Look at the diagram below which shows a basic solar heating system. Then look at the notes below the diagram. Use these notes to write a paragraph describing how the system works. Try to use passive forms of verbs where appropriate. Do not forget to supply articles. The first and last sentences of the paragraph are given to help you.

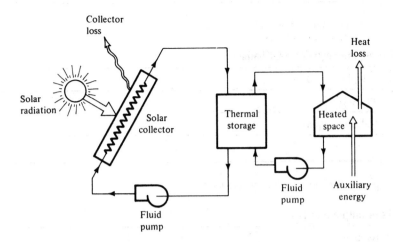

A simple solar heating system is shown in the diagram above.

- First, solar radiation / absorbed /solar collector.
- Some energy / lost / reflected / to sky.
- Liquid in collector / heated / sun's energy.
- Next, heated liquid / carried / thermal store.
- Thermal storage / required if energy / needed when no solar radiation / available.
- Often, storage tank / heating element / increase temperature.
- Hot liquid / pumped / area where / needed.
- In most buildings, heat / lost / roof so auxiliary heat / used.
- Cool liquid / returned to tank and then to solar collector / pumps.

Engineers need to be able to calculate the potential for a solar heating system and to be aware of the possibility of using solar energy in installations.

C. Listening

Listen to your tape. You will hear part of a lecture on the subject of the potential of solar heating systems for use in family homes. As you listen, complete the chart below with the missing information. The lecture is divided into sections to help you.

Section 1

- What has the first part of the lecture been about?

- Complete the chart below with the missing facts.

Houses with solar heating domestic hot water

Country/area	Number/ratio
W. Europe	
	1 in 60
Italy	
	1 in 300
UK/W. Germany	
	1 in 20

▼

Section 2

- Complete the chart below with the missing facts.

Typical requirements for a UK family

Average number in house

Hot water usage

Size of collector required

Section 3

- Complete this chart with the missing facts.

Details of output and cost

Water usage

Average temp. of water

Solar collector area

Gain from solar collector

Installation cost, 1982

Section 4

- What material are solar cells made from?
- What is the efficiency of a solar cell?
- What word describes the potential use of solar energy?

A. Understanding a printed text (1)

Read the following text. As you read, look for the information to answer these questions. Remember, you do not have to understand all the words to answer the questions.

1. What is the vapour-compression cycle?
2. What are its applications?
3. Can the Carnot refrigeration cycle be used in industrial processes today?
4. How does the actual cycle differ from the standard cycle?

Most important refrigeration cycle

1 The vapor-compression cycle is the most widely used refrigeration cycle in practice. In this cycle a vapor is compressed, then condensed to a liquid, following which the pressure is dropped so that fluid can evaporate at a low pressure.

Carnot refrigeration cycle

2 The Carnot cycle is one whose efficiency cannot be exceeded when operating between two given temperatures. The Carnot cycle operating as a heat engine is familiar from the study of thermodynamics. The Carnot heat engine receives energy at a high level of temperature, converts a portion of the energy into work, and discharges the remainder to a heat sink at a low level of temperature.

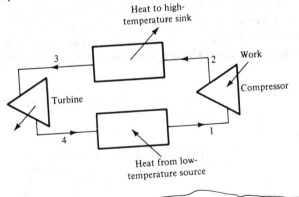

Figure 1. The vapour-compression cycle.

3 The Carnot refrigeration cycle performs the reverse effect of the heat engine because it transfers energy from a low level of temperature to a high level of temperature. The refrigeration cycle requires the addition of external work for its operation. The diagram of the equipment of the refrigeration cycle is shown in Figure 1.

4   The processes which constitute the cycle are:
1–2 COMPRESSION
2–3 REJECTION OF HEAT
3–4 EXPANSION
4–1 ADDITION OF HEAT
All the processes of the Carnot cycle are thermodynamically reversible.

5   The withdrawal of heat from the low-temperature source in process 4–1 is the refrigeration step and is the entire purpose of the cycle. All other processes in the cycle function so that the low-temperature energy can be discharged to some convenient high-temperature heat sink.

6   The Carnot cycle consists of reversible processes which make its efficiency higher than could be achieved in an actual cycle. A reasonable question is this: Why discuss the Carnot cycle if it is an unattainable ideal? There are two reasons: (1) it serves as a standard of comparison, and (2) it provides a convenient guide to the temperatures that should be maintained to achieve maximum effectiveness.

The standard cycle and the actual cycle

7   Because the Carnot refrigeration cycle is the most efficient cycle, every attempt should be made to reproduce it with actual equipment. Modifications to the cycle are dictated by practical considerations. Certainly the reversible processes cannot be reproduced, but several revisions can be made which achieve an effective result. These revisions mainly involve changes to the compression and expansion processes. For example: (1) the fluid which enters the compression must be in the form of dry vapor because liquid can damage the compressor. This results in a higher temperature at point 2 in the cycle, however. (2) An expansion valve is used instead of a turbine to reduce the pressure of the liquid so that it can evaporate at low pressure in the evaporator. The result is the standard vapor-compression cycle which is a modified version of the Carnot cycle.

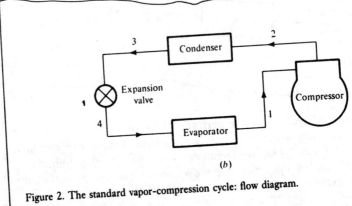

(b)

Figure 2. The standard vapor-compression cycle: flow diagram.

8   The actual vapor compression cycle is inefficient in comparison with the standard cycle. The essential difference is that the standard cycle assumes no drop in pressure in the condenser and evaporator. In the actual cycle, however, the pressure of the refrigerant drops because of friction. The result of these drops in pressure is that the compression process (1–2) requires more work than the standard cycle.

W.F. Stoecker & J.J. Jones. *Refrigeration and Air Conditioning*, pp 187–190. McGraw-Hill, 1982.

B. Check your understanding

Now read the text again carefully. While you read, look for the answers to these questions.

1. Mark the following sentences true of false, according to the information given in the text:

● The Carnot cycle is the most efficient when operating between two given temperatures. ☐

● The Carnot cycle can be applied to both heat engines and refrigeration. ☐

● The refrigeration cycle can operate independently of external sources of work. ☐

● In the second stage (process 2–3), heat is transferred from the environment to the system. ☐

● If there is liquid in the vapour as it enters the compressor, this can be harmful to the compressor. ☐

● The actual cycle is more efficient than the standard cycle. ☐

● In the standard cycle, the pressure of the liquid is low as it leaves the condenser. ☐

● In the actual cycle, friction causes the pressure to fall in the condenser and evaporator. ☐

2. Given that the Carnot refrigeration cycle has the reverse effect of the heat engine, can you redraw Figure 1 so that it represents the Carnot heat engine?

These statements will help you:

1. Vapour is compressed, and the cycle starts (again).
2. Heat is taken from a high temperature outside source.
3. Part of the energy is used to drive a turbine and produce work.
4. The other part is discharged to an outside area which has a low level of temperature.

3. In the chart below, write the numbers 1, 2, 3 and 4 in the appropriate boxes corresponding to the four points of the vapour-compression cycle to indicate the state of the refrigerant at each point.

	High pressure	Low pressure
Gas		
Liquid		

C. Increase your vocabulary

Remember that you can use a dictionary to help you answer these questions.

1. Find the words in the text which mean the same as the following:

- go above / be better than (paragraph 2)
- take / accept (2)
- change (from one form to another) (2)
- release / emit (2)
- carry out (3)
- make a copy / duplicate (7)

2. (a) Complete the table by writing the noun or adjective forms of the verbs and adjectives given. ('X' indicates that you need not write anything here.)

Noun	Verb	Adjective
1.	withdraw	X
2.	X	efficient
3.	modify	X
4.	add	additional
5. X	attain	
6.	reproduce	X
7. reversal	reverse	

(b) Now write the negative forms of the adjectives given at 2, 5 and 7 in the table.

3. Explain the underlined words and phrases:

- operating between two <u>given</u> temperatures
- converts <u>a portion</u> of the energy into work
- discharged to some <u>convenient</u> high temperature <u>heat sink</u>
- the <u>entire</u> purpose of the cycle
- maximum <u>effectiveness</u>
- <u>dictated</u> by practical considerations
- the <u>essential</u> difference

D. Check your grammar

1. COMPARING

Notice these ways to make comparisons:

- *Both* the Carnot cycle *and* the standard cycle involve the processes of compression and expansion.

- *Neither* the Carnot cycle *nor* the standard cycle can be reproduced with actual equipment.

  - *In comparison with*
  - *Compared with*   the standard cycle, the actual cycle is less efficient.

Now write two sentences about each of the following. Say, first, what two things they have in common (Both / Neither) and second, how they compare (e.g. which is faster, more economical etc.)

- Steam trains and diesel trains
- Gasoline and diesel engines in cars
- Iron and stainless steel
- Metals and plastics
- Oxygen and hydrogen

2. *CONTRASTING*

Look at these examples:

- The Carnot cycle assumes the use of a turbine *while*
  whereas the standard cycle uses an expansion valve.
- The standard cycle assumes no drop in pressure in the condenser and evaporator. In the actual cycle, *however,*
  on the other hand, the pressure drops because of friction.

Now, write a sentence (or sentences) to contrast each of the following, using *while*, *whereas*, *however* or *on the other hand*.

- Hammer / screwdriver
- Air-cooled engines / water-cooled engines
- Solids / fluids
- Gases / liquids
- Thermal conduction / convection

3. *EXPRESSING ADVANTAGES AND DISADVANTAGES*

Look at these examples:

- *The advantage of* the dry vapour system *is that* it will not damage the compressor.
- *The disadvantage of* feeding dry vapour to the compressor *is that* a higher temperature results.

Now decide whether the feature supplied for each 'subject' is an advantage or a disadvantage. Then write a sentence about it.

Subject	Feature
• The Carnot cycle	serves as a standard of comparison
• Diesel engines	need a lot of maintenance
• Frozen foods	can be stored for long periods
• Floppy disks	can be damaged easily
• Diesel engines	require no ignition system
• Alternative sources of energy	are expensive to develop

E. Understanding a lecture

You will hear part of a lecture. It has been divided into three sections, representing extracts from a longer lecture. The first section is taken from the beginning of the lecture; the second part from the middle and the third part from near the end.

As you listen, take notes and then see if you can use your notes to answer the following questions.

1. ● What is a refrigerant?
   ● What two important characteristics of refrigerants are mentioned in Section 2?
   ● Would ammonia be suitable for use in freezing food, do you think?
   ● How does ammonia compare with refrigerant 12? [Give figures if you can.]

2. Complete the table for refrigerants mentioned in the lecture:

Refrigerant	Characteristics	Applications
Air		
Ammonia	Large refrigerating effect	
	Suitable for the low-temperature side of a two-section system	
	Can be used with a small, low-cost compressor	

3. Listen to the lecture again and try to find the answers to these questions.

(a) The lecture consists of three main sections. What does each section deal with?

(b) ● How does the lecturer begin the lecture? What words does he use?
    ● How does he begin the third section?
    ● What other words can you find which tell you about the *order* of points in the lecture?

F. Understanding a printed text (2)

Condensers and Evaporators

Condensers and evaporators as heat exchangers
Since both the condenser and the evaporator are heat exchangers, they have certain features in common. One classification of condensers and evaporators (see Table 1) is according to whether the refrigerant is on the inside or outside of the tubes and whether the fluid cooling the condenser or being refrigerated is a gas or a liquid. The gas referred to in the table is usually air and the liquid is usually water, but other substances are used as well.

Table 1 Some types of evaporators and condensers

Component	Refrigerant	Fluid
Condenser	Inside tubes	Gas outside Liquid outside†
	Outside tubes	Gas inside† Liquid inside
Evaporator	Inside tubes	Gas outside Liquid outside
	Outside tubes	Gas inside† Liquid inside

† Seldom used.

The most widely used types of condensers and evaporators are shell-and-tube heat exchangers (Figure A) and finned-coil heat exchangers. The Table indicates that certain combinations are not frequently used, particularly the configuration where the gas is passed through tubes. The reason is that volume flow rates of gases are high relative to those of liquids and would result in high pressure drops if forced through the tubes.

Figure A. Shell-and-tube water-cooled condenser. *(ITT Bell & Gossett — Fluid Handling Division.)*

Condensers For the condenser, the fluid to which heat is rejected is usually either air or water. When the condenser is water-cooled, the water is sent to a cooling tower for ultimate rejection of the heat to the atmosphere. Some years ago air-cooled condensers were used only in small refrigeration systems (less than 100 kW refrigerating capacity), but now individual air-cooled condensers are manufactured in sizes matching refrigeration capacities of hundreds of kilowatts. The water-cooled condenser is favored over the air-cooled condenser where there is a long distance between the compressor and the point where heat is to be rejected. Most designers prefer to convey water rather than refrigerant in long lines.

Evaporators   In most refrigerating evaporators the refrigerant boils in the tubes and cools the fluid that passes over the outside of the tubes. Evaporators that boil refrigerant in the tubes are often called direct expansion evaporators. Direct expansion evaporators used for air-conditioning applications are usually fed by an expansion valve that regulates the flow of liquid so that the refrigerant vapor leaves the evaporator with some superheat, as shown in Figure F(a). Another concept is the liquid-recirculation or liquid-overfeed evaporator in Figure F(b) in which excess liquid at low pressure and temperature is pumped to the evaporator. Some liquid boils in the evaporator, and the remainder floods out of the outlet. The liquid from the evaporator is separated out, and vapor flows on to the compressor. Low temperature industrial refrigeration systems often use this type of evaporator. The advantage is that the heat transfer is very efficient.

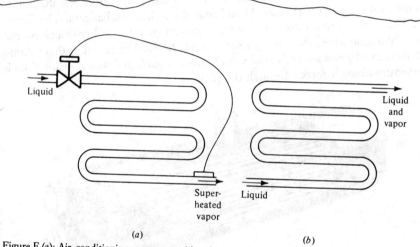

Liquid

Liquid and vapor

Super-heated vapor

Liquid

(a)

(b)

Figure F (a); Air-conditioning evaporator with refrigerant leaving in a superheated state, (b) liquid-recirculation evaporator with liquid refrigerant carried out of the evaporator.

While refrigerant boils inside the tubes of most commercial evaporators, in one important class of liquid-chilling evaporator the refrigerant boils outside the tubes. This type of evaporator is used in conjunction with reciprocating compressors, but in such applications provision must be made for returning oil to the compressor. In the evaporators where refrigerant boils in the tubes, the velocity of the refrigerant vapor is maintained high enough to carry oil back to the compressor.

W.F. Stoecker & J.J. Jones. *Refrigeration and Air Conditioning*, pp 233–4, 243–4. McGraw-Hill, 1982.

G. Check your understanding

1. Make a list of all the different types of condenser and evaporator mentioned in the text.

2. Now match certain types of condenser/evaporator in your list with the features or applications listed below on the right.

Type of condenser/evaporator	Feature/application
(a)	Water sent to the cooling tower and heat rejected to the atmosphere.
(b)	Once used only in small refrigeration systems.
(c)	Used where there is a long distance between the compressor and point of heat rejection.
(d)	Have an expansion valve which regulates the flow of liquid.
(e)	Used in low temperature industrial refrigeration systems.
(f)	The refrigerant boils outside the tubes.
(g)	Is used in conjunction with reciprocating compressors.

3. Now tick all the following statements which are correct:

(a) Gas is rarely passed inside the tubes of evaporators and condensers. □
(b) Liquids have a relatively higher flow rate than gases. □
(c) It is thought that water can be better transported over long distances than refrigerant. □
(d) Centrifugal compression systems are usually combined with water-cooled condensers. □
(e) The liquid recirculation evaporator is commonly used in air-conditioning applications. □
(f) In evaporators where the refrigerant boils outside the tubes, oil is carried to the compressor by the velocity of the refrigerant vapour. □

H. Understanding discourse

Listen to your tape. You will hear part of a discussion where a man, Tim, is putting forward an idea for a new kind of heating system. Listen carefully to the system he describes and to the questions other members of the group ask. Listen to the tape a second time. Then complete the exercise below.

1. ● What does the first speaker do at the beginning of the meeting?
   ● What is the purpose of the meeting?
   ● How often does the group meet?

2. ● Working in a group if you think this is useful, draw a simple diagram of Tim's idea. Then explain it to the rest of the class.

3. ● What additional idea is suggested by someone in the group?
   ● What disadvantage of the system is suggested?
   ● What is the group going to do as the tape fades?

4. (a). Notice the form of this question:
   It could absorb heat from water too, couldn't it?
   Write down two more examples of this type of question which you heard in the discussion.
   ● ....
   ● ....

   (b) Now write down the correct question ending in the sentences below.
   ● You are studying engineering .... ?
   ● The system would be expensive .... ?
   ● The system needs special pipes .... ?
   ● They will finish at 10 o'clock .... ?
   ● You don't live on campus... ?

A. Understanding a printed text (1)

The following text gives an introduction to the practice of **chlorinating water** for the purpose of disinfecting it. As you read the text, look for the answers to these questions. Remember, you do not have to understand all the words to answer the questions.

1. What can happen as a result of chlorination?
2. What are the four main purposes of chlorinating water?
3. Do we know for certain how chlorine acts on bacteria?
4. What is meant by the terms: (a) plain chlorination; (b) prechlorination; (c) postchlorination?

People need water which is clear and free from disease-causing organisms. They also desire water which is soft, free from tastes and odors, and does not discolor plumbing fixtures or corrode metals. Industry requires water that will not interfere with its processes. Recently there has been increasing concern about the presence of minute quantities of organic material, particularly chlorinated hydrocarbons, which are thought to be causative agents of a variety of diseases. Such contaminants are known to be present in many water supplies although their effect upon health is unknown. Standard disinfection practice using chlorine contributes to the production of these compounds.

Chlorine in water

Disinfection of water is the killing of disease-causing microorganisms that it may contain. In the process, bacteria are reduced in number. Complete sterilization, however, is not ordinarily obtained nor necessary. Chlorine in its various forms has been widely used in disinfecting water. It is cheap, reliable and presents no great difficulty in handling.

Chlorine is a very active element and when added to water as free chlorine it will combine with organic and inorganic matter and oxidize some organic and inorganic compounds. Free available chlorine reacts with ammonia and many organic amines to form chloramines. The chlorine in water in chemical combination with ammonia or other nitrogenous compounds which modify its rate of bactericidal action is known as the combined available chlorine. The chlorine demand of water is the difference between the amount of chlorine present as a residual, either free or combined, after some designated period.

Chlorine is used in water treatment for disinfection, prevention and destruction of odors, iron removal and color removal. While its principal use is as a disinfectant the mechanism of its bactericidal action is uncertain. It is likely that the chlorine destroys the extracellular enzymes of the bacterial cells, and possible that it actually passes through the cell wall to attack intracellular systems. The bactericidal efficiency of chlorine is reduced by increased pH values and low temperatures.

Chlorination

Chlorination of water is practised for the purposes listed above and the various needs may be satisfied simultaneously. Chlorine is classified according to its point of application and its end result.

Plain chlorination In some cities surface waters are used with no other treatment than chlorination, although in some of these cities long storage is also given. In such cases, chlorination is extremely important as the principal if not the only safeguard against disease. Such otherwise untreated waters are likely to be rather high in inorganic matter and require high dosages and long contact periods for maximum safety. The chlorine may be added to the water in the pipe leading from an impounding reservoir to the city. For disinfection alone a dose of 0.5 mg/l or more may be required to obtain a combined available residual in the city distribution system.

Prechlorination This is the application of chlorine before any other treatment. The chlorine may be added in the suction pipes of raw-water pumps or to the water as it enters the mixing chamber. Its use in this manner has several advantages. It may improve coagulation and will reduce tastes and odors caused by organic sludge in the sedimentation tank. By reducing algae and other organisms it may keep the filter sand cleaner and increase the length of filter runs. Its range of effective action will, of course, depend upon the maintenance of a residual through the units of the plant. Frequently the dosage is such that a combined available residual of 0.1 to 0.5 mg/l goes to the filters. The combination of prechlorination with postchlorination may be advisable or even necessary if the raw water is very highly polluted.

Postchlorination This usually refers to the addition of chlorine to the water after all other treatments. The chlorine may be added in the suction line of the service pump, but it is preferable to add it in the filter effluent pipe or in the clear well so that an adequate contact time will be assured. This should be at least 30 minutes before any of the water is consumed if only postchlorination is given. Dosage will depend upon the character of the water and may be 0.25 to 0.5 mg/l in order to obtain a combined available residue of 0.1 to 0.2 mg/l as the water leaves the plant. Greater residuals will probably be needed if it is desired to hold a disinfecting effect throughout the distribution system. This is considered desirable since it affords protection against contamination from cross connections and prevents organic growths in mains and their resulting odors.

Steel & McGhee. *Water Supply and Sewerage*, pp 274–276. McGraw-Hill, 1979.

B. Check your understanding

Now read the text more carefully. While you read, look for the answers to these questions:

1. What properties should a good water supply have?

2. What is one kind of organic material, present in many water supplies, which is thought to cause disease?

3. What two factors can reduce the efficiency of chlorine as a bactericide?

4. If chlorine is the only water treatment used, what must be done to ensure that the water is safe?

5. What is the combined available residual referred to in the text? Can you explain in your own words?

6. What are the three main advantages of prechlorination?

7. What action is recommended if the raw water is highly polluted?

8. How much contact time is needed before water can be drunk if only postchlorination is given?

9. In postchlorination, what combined available residual should the water have as it leaves the treatment plant?

10. Are greater residuals than this sometimes needed? Why?

C. Increase your vocabulary

Remember, you can use a dictionary to help you answer these questions.

1. Find the words in the text which can be used to replace those underlined below:

- The public <u>requires</u> that their water supply be clean and safe to drink.

- There has been some <u>anxiety</u> about organic materials which could cause disease.

- Chlorine <u>kills</u> the extracellular enzymes of bacterial cells.

- Prechlorination in combination with postchlorination is often <u>recommended</u> if the raw water is very polluted.

- It is <u>better</u> to add chlorine to the filter effluent pipe rather than in the suction line of the service pump.

- Greater residuals <u>provide a safeguard</u> against contamination from cross connections.

2. Correct the sentences below by replacing the underlined words with a word or words from the text which will have the opposite meaning.

- Industry requires water that will <u>have an effect on</u> its processes.
- <u>Large</u> quantities of organic material are found in mains water.
- Chlorinated hydrocarbons are <u>absent</u> in the water supply.
- Standard disinfection practice <u>prevents</u> the production of these compounds.
- The bactericidal efficiency of chlorine is <u>increased</u> by increased pH values.
- Chlorine is used in water treatment for disinfection, destruction of odours and iron <u>addition</u>.

3. Verbs and nouns. Write the missing forms into the table.

Verb	Noun
● add	
● apply	
●	destruction
● treat	
●	action
●	combination
● consume	
●	corrosion

4. Double noun forms.

There are often two noun forms which have the same stem but rather different meanings. Decide which form is correct in each of the following sentences:

- Chlorine is commonly used as a DISINFECTION / DISINFECTANT.
- For DISINFECTION / DISINFECTANT, a DOSE / DOSAGE of 0.5 mg/l of chlorine must be added to the water supply.
- A higher DOSE / DOSAGE may be required to prevent CONTAMINATION / CONTAMINANT throughout the distribution system.
- In the SEDIMENTATION / SEDIMENT tank, particles of SEDIMENTATION / SEDIMENT are removed by horizontal scrapers.

D. Check your grammar

1. CAUSE/AFFECT

Look at these examples:

- Chlorinated hydrocarbons may *cause* a variety of diseases.
- Increased pH values *affect* the bactericidal efficiency of chlorine.

Now complete these sentences:

1. Contaminants in the water
   supply .... the health of people who drink it.

2. Using chlorine as a
   disinfectant .... the production of harmful
   compounds.

3. Low water temperatures .... the efficiency of chlorine as a
   bactericide.

4. Prechlorination .... the reduction of algae and other
   organisms.

5. The chlorine dosage .... the combined available residual
   in the water distribution system.

2. POSSIBILITY, PROBABILITY AND CERTAINTY

Notice these ways to express different degrees of possibility, probability and certainty:

i. *Certainty:* *It is certain that* dirty water causes disease
   It is known that . . .
   Dirty water *will* cause disease.

ii. *Probability:* *It is likely that* untreated water is high in organic matter.
   Untreated water *will probably* be high in organic matter.

iii. *Possibility:* *It is possible that* prechlorination improves coagulation.
   Prechlorination *may possibly* improve coagulation.

iv. *Improbability:* *It is unlikely that* highly polluted water can be effectively treated by
   prechlorination alone.
   Highly polluted water *will probably not* be treated effectively by
   prechlorination alone.

Now express the following sentences in the same way. The number given with each sentence indicates whether you should express *certainty, probability, possibility* or *improbability*.

- Effective water treatment results in a decrease in disease. (ii)
- Chlorine destroys the extracellular enzymes of bacterial cells. (ii)
- Chlorine also attacks the intracellular systems of bacteria. (iii)
- Complete sterilisation of water can be obtained. (iv)
- The use of lead pipes to carry drinking water can lead to lead poisoning. (i)
- Both prechlorination and postchlorination will be needed if the water is highly polluted. (ii)
- Prechlorination helps to keep the filter sand clean. (iii)
- A cure for all diseases will be found. (iv)

▼

Look at these examples:

- The combination of prechlorination and postchlorination *is advised/ is recommended*
  or less certain: /*may be advisable*

- *It is recommended that chlorine is* added to the suction line.
  It is recommended that chlorine *should be* added to the suction line.

  or less certain:

  It is preferable to add chlorine to the suction line.

Now express each of the following as a recommendation:

- Filtration should be used in water treatment.
- Fourteen filter units should be built to treat 23,000 m³/day.
- Chlorine gas treatment should replace the old chlorinated lime method.
- Where chlorine gas is stored, adequate ventilation should be provided.
- Store gas cylinders at temperatures below 15°C.
- Use chloramines as a bactericide in water treatment.

E. Understanding a lecture

Listen to the lecture which is about filtration in water treatment. In the lecture, the diagram below is referred to.

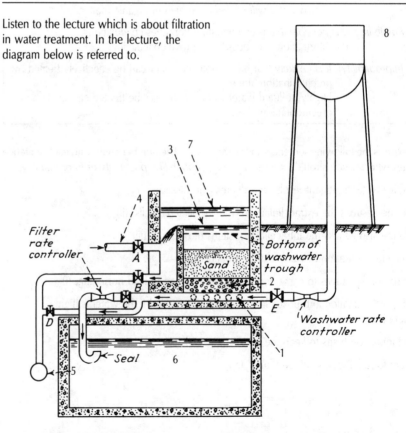

Figure 10-2 Diagrammatic section of a rapid sand gravity filter. A, B, C, D, and E are valves, which may be hydraulically or pneumatically actuated. Valve D permits wasting filtered water. The seal in the effluent pipe keeps the pipe full at all times so that the rate controller will function.

1. Match the labels below with the numbers on Figure 10–2.

Water from settling basin ..
Water level during filtration ..
Layer of gravel ..
Drain ..
Filtered water storage tank ..
Washwater storage tank ..
Water level during washing ..
Washwater drain ..

2. Now answer these questions:

- Why is filtration necessary?
- What type of filtration process is described by the lecturer?
- What are the advantages of this process?
- What is the term used to describe water that has a lot of particles in suspension?
- What are the three characteristics that distinguish the rapid filter?
- What filter medium is commonly used in rapid filters such as the one described in the lecture?

3. Give a brief description in your own words of:

   (a) Filtration in a rapid sand gravity filter.
   (b) Washing the filters.

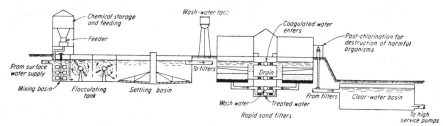

Figure 10-1 Filtration plant, including coagulation, settling, filtration, postchlorination and clear-water storage. Prechlorination, i.e., addition of chlorine at the mixing basin, is also common practice.

F. Understanding a printed text (2)

The following text is a report written by a geologist to a township council which needs additional water supplies.

Foreword

Within Milton Township, the greatest industrial and residential development has occurred in areas with limited groundwater resources. This development has already created water shortages and a need to deepen existing wells; more seriously, it has greatly handicapped or prevented the development of new industry. Thus, the township council authorised Moody and Associates to locate, if possible, several high-yield water wells to provide a sufficient municipal water supply. The purpose of this report is to describe the successful location of sand and gravel materials with excellent groundwater yielding capacity.

Summary

We conducted studies and six test drillings to locate an area in which a reliable high-quality, municipal water well field could be developed. We have located such a site.

CONCLUSIONS: Production wells completed at the test well sites should more than supply the township's current and future needs. Analyses of test data indicate that such production wells could produce over 2 million gallons per day, twice the township's projected requirements. Further, if the water-bearing sand and gravel are as extensive as we project them to be, yields up to 5 million gallons per day could conceivably be developed.

RECOMMENDATION: We recommend that the property tested be acquired for development as a municipal well field. The property is unique in its supply capability within Milton Township, and a well field on this property should meet any present and foreseeable water requirements within the township.

RESULTS: Four of the six wells drilled were productive and penetrated sand and gravel suitable for development of municipal wells. Each of the four productive wells showed very good water-producing capability, yielding 300 to 500 gallons per minute. Further, the wells produced water of generally excellent quality though with a potentially high but treatable concentration of manganese. One test well showed manganese concentration now high enough to require treatment, and there is concern that manganese levels in all the wells might increase to such a level. However, this would not prevent development of the well field and additional study will be required to determine if manganese removal is necessary at all.

Huckin & Olsen. *English for Science and Technology.* McGraw-Hill, 1983.

G. Check your understanding

1. Answer the following questions:

- What problem did the people of Milton Township have with their water supply?
- Was this also a problem for local industry?
- What job did the local council give Moody and Associates?
- Did Moody complete the job successfully?
- How many productive test wells were drilled and how much water did they each yield?
- Was there any problem concerning the quality of this water?

2. In the following questions, choose the most accurate statement according to the information given in the text:

A (a) Treatment for manganese removal will certainly be required.
   (b) Treatment for manganese removal will probably be required.
   (c) Treatment for manganese removal will possibly be required.
   (d) Treatment for manganese removal is unlikely to be required.

B (a) The completed production wells are certain to supply the town's present and future needs.
   (b) The completed production wells are likely to supply the town's present and future needs.
   (c) It is possible that the completed production wells will supply the town's present and future needs.
   (d) The completed production wells are unlikely to supply the town's present and future needs.

C (a) Yields up to 5 million gallons per day will be developed.
   (b) Yields up to 5 million gallons per day will probably be developed.
   (c) Yields up to 5 million gallons per day are possible.
   (d) Yields up to 5 million gallons per day are unlikely.

D The writer recommends:
   (a) The Township should definitely buy the site for development as a well field.
   (b) The Township should consider buying the site.
   (c) The Township should buy the site if further tests prove favourable.
   (d) The Township should not buy the site.

H. Understanding discourse

You will hear a conversation between a representative of the Milton Township, Mr Hacker, and Mr Moody, who wrote the report you have just read. Mr Hacker is asking some questions about the report and Mr Moody replies, giving advice and recommendations.

When you have listened to the conversation, write down three recommendations made by Mr Moody. Express the recommendations formally, as in the examples given in Section D.3.

A. Understanding a printed text (1)

The following text gives you an introduction to the **use of satellites for communication purposes**. As you read, look for answers to the following questions. Remember, you do not have to understand every word in order to answer the questions.

1. What services, mentioned in the text, do communications satellites provide?

2. What are the two satellite systems which communications engineers have had to choose between?

3. Which system has been the most widely used?

4. What organisation operates over a dozen satellites with global coverage?

5. In what circumstances does the need for a regional satellite system arise?

15–3.2 Satellite Communications

A communications satellite receives the energy beamed up at it by an earth station and amplifies and returns it to earth at a frequency of about 2 gigahertz away; this prevents interference between the uplink and the downlink. Communications satellites appear to hover over given spots above the equator. This does not make them stationary, but rather *geostationary*. That is to say, they have the same angular velocity as the Earth (i.e. one complete cycle per 24 hours), and so they appear to be stationed over one spot on the globe. Celestial mechanics shows that a satellite orbiting the Earth will do so at a velocity that depends on its distance from the Earth, and on whether the satellite is in a circular or an elliptical orbit. For example, a satellite in a low circular orbit, as was *Sputnik I*, will orbit the Earth in 90 minutes. The moon, which is nearly 385,000 km away, orbits in 28 days. A satellite in circular orbit 35,800 km away from the earth will complete a revolution in 24 hours, as does the Earth below it, and this is why it *appears* stationary.[5]

Whether to use a stationary satellite or a succession of satellites in low, elliptical orbits for global communications is a question that exercised the minds of communications engineers in the early 1960s. It was really a case of convenience versus distance, and convenience won. That is to say, satellites in close elliptical orbits require relatively low transmitting powers and receiver sensitivities but must be tracked by the antennas of the ground stations. Stationary satellites present no tracking problems but are so far away that large antennas, high powers and high receiver sensitivities are essential. With the sole exception of the USSR's *Molniya* satellite system, all other communications satellites use the synchronous orbits which all but eliminate satellite tracking.

The major communications satellite systems include those operated by INTELSAT, whose satellites are used for global point-to-point communications, INMARSAT, which serves a similar role for ships at sea; and finally the various regional and domestic satellite systems being operated in a number of regions or by individual countries.

INTELSAT satellites   COMSAT (Communications Satellite Corporation) of the United States, the Overseas Telecommunications Commission (Australia) and nine other world communications agencies met in Washington, D.C., in 1964, to sign a document that made them founder members of the International Telecommunications Satellite Consortium (i.e., INTELSAT). When *INTELSAT 1*, better known as *Early Bird*, was launched over the Atlantic in 1965, there were just five earth stations to make use of the 66 telephone circuits it offered. Today, there are over one dozen *INTELSAT IV, IV-A, V* and *VA* satellites in the Atlantic, Indian and Pacific Ocean regions, offering capacities up to 12,500 two-way telephone circuits and two one-way TV channels per satellite. The *INTELSAT VI* satellites, expected to be launched in the late 1980s, will be capable of providing up to 20,000 telephone circuits each. Over 500 earth stations in nearly 150 countries make use of the *INTELSAT* satellites in the three ocean regions to provide over 25,000 circuits and TV services for international and domestic use.

Regional and domestic satellites   As the name suggests, a regional satellite system is a kind of mini-INTELSAT designed to serve a region with community interests, especially in communications. The world's first regional satellite system was the Indonesian *Palapa* network, inaugurated in the mid-1970s, initially for domestic services (Indonesia consists of over 3000 islands, with some 1800 of them inhabited), but by the late 1970s it had expanded to neighboring countries such as the Philippines. The Conference of European Post and Telegraph Administration (CEPT) was next on the scene, with EUTELSAT created in the early 1980s, under the auspices of the European Space Agency (ESA), whose other main function is the development and operation of the *Ariane* satellite launcher (used by a number of organizations, including INTELSAT). EUTELSAT provides and maintains the space segment for the European Communication Satellite (ECS), and individual countries provide their own earth stations, as with INTELSAT.

The ECS system came into service in 1983, operating in the 14/12-GHz band, with ground antennas very much like the INTELSAT standard C antennas, but with lower ground and satellite transmit powers. The system is used for intra-European telephone, data and telex/telegraph services, and also by the European Broadcasting Union, for the distribution of its *EUROVISION* programs.

Another regional satellite system to go into service has been ARABSAT, which is used by countries in the Middle East.

There is conceptually not a great deal of difference between a regional satellite system used by a group of neighboring countries and a domestic system used by a large or dispersed country. Indeed, they share a common characteristic which makes them quite different from the global INTELSAT system, in requiring a much smaller coverage area. Each INTELSAT satellite must have a beam accessible to roughly one-third of the globe, resulting in a coverage of almost exactly 170 million km^2. On the other hand, a circular beam could cover the whole of India, for example, if it had a radius on the ground of 1450 km. The resulting 6.6-million-km^2-coverage area represents a 26-fold reduction when compared to the global beam. All else being equal, it means that the satellite antenna gain can, in this case, be increased by a factor of 26. The result is a very significant gain increase compared with the global system, and consequently much smaller receiving antennas and simpler receivers on the ground.

Although the conceptual difference between a regional and a domestic satellite system is not great, the *political* difference is enormous! No international conferences are needed; there are no language barriers, no requirements to correlate different national technical standards (making the usual compromises), no necessity to make allowances for the least developed entity in the group, and so on (students will gather from all this that the author speaks from long personal experience!). Moreover, in all the world's countries except one (the United States) there is just one satellite organization, normally government-owned, so that even domestic friction is avoided. It should come as no surprise, therefore, that domestic satellite systems preceded regional ones by several years and, as might be expected, North America led the field.

[5]The actual orbital *velocity of a geostationary satellite is 11,000 km/ per hour, or nearly 2 mi per second.*

G. Kennedy. *Electronic Communication Systems*, pp 560–561. McGraw-Hill, 1985.

B. Check your understanding

Now read the text more carefully. While you read, look for the answers to these questions:

1. Find the best item to complete each sentence according to the information given in the text.

● A geostationary satellite . . .

   (a) is motionless in space (except for its spin).
   (b) is not really stationary at all, but orbits the Earth within a 24-hour period.
   (c) appears stationary over the Earth's magnetic pole.
   (d) is located at a height of 35,800 km to ensure global coverage.

- A satellite in synchronous orbit . . .

  (a) must be tracked by the antennas of ground stations.
  (b) requires relatively low transmitting powers.
  (c) presents no tracking problems.
  (d) has a low circular orbit.

- INTELSAT . . .

  (a) provides both two-way phone circuits and one-way TV channels.
  (b) provides point-to-point communication for ships.
  (c) was formed when nine world communications agencies signed an agreement in 1964.
  (d) is an international communication satellite system.

- Regional satellites . . .

  (a) require a smaller coverage area than INTELSAT satellites.
  (b) can only be utilised by nations that have a common language.
  (c) , so far, have only been developed for use by the European Community.
  (d) operate on an entirely different system from domestic satellites.

- Domestic satellites . . .

  (a) require careful correlation of different national technical standards.
  (b) came into use before regional satellites.
  (c) without exception are government-owned.
  (d) require the same ground equipment as INTELSAT satellites.

2. Tick all the statements from the list below which are true:

(a) The velocity with which a satellite orbits the earth depends on its distance from the earth. ☐
(b) Sputnik 1 had an elliptical orbit. ☐
(c) Satellites in low elliptical orbits do not require high receiver sensitivities. ☐
(d) Early Bird was the name of the first communications satellite to be launched. ☐
(e) INTELSAT V offers a capacity of 12,500 two-way phone circuits. ☐
(f) INTELSAT VI was launched in the early 1980s. ☐
(g) More than 500 countries make use of INTELSAT satellite communications. ☐
(h) The Indonesian satellite system was originally developed to serve domestic purposes. ☐
(i) A beam which has a coverage of about 6.5 million square kilometres is adequate for regional or domestic purposes. ☐
(j) The satellite antenna for a regional satellite system has to be 26 times bigger than that of an INTELSAT satellite. ☐

3. What do the underlined words and phrases refer to in these sentences taken from the text:

- A communications satellite receives the energy beamed up at it by an Earth station and amplifies and returns it to Earth at a frequency of about 2 gigahertz away; this prevents interference between the uplink and the downlink.

- Celestial mechanics shows that a satellite orbiting the Earth will do so at a velocity that depends on its distance from the Earth.

▼

C. Increase your vocabulary

Remember that you can use a dictionary to help you answer these questions.

1. Match the words on the left, which are from the text, with a word or phrase that has the same meaning from the list on the right.

- appear   particular place
- precede   grow bigger
- expand   seem
- sole   to begin with
- convenience   come before
- inaugurate   freedom from problems
- spot   only
- initially   to have its beginning

2. Notice how these verbs are used in the text. Then choose the correct one to complete each sentence below. Be careful to use the correct form of the verb.

- eliminate   • present   • provide
- serve   • share

- Many countries _____ the benefits of the INTELSAT satellite service.

- Satellite systems help to _____ services for remote communities.

- The Palapa network _____ the Indonesian islands and some of its neighbours such as the Philippines.

- Satellite communications _____ an alternative to terrestrial links such as cable networks.

- Domestic satellite systems _____ the need for the correlating of different national technical standards.

D. Check your grammar

1. COMPARING AND CONTRASTING

Look at these examples:

Contrasting (not like; ≠)

- Domestic systems *are quite different from INTELSAT*.

- Domestic systems can be set up without compromising needs, *whereas* regional systems have to serve many different requirements.

- Domestic systems, *unlike* regional systems, can be set up without compromising needs.

Comparing (like; =)

- *Compared with* the global system, domestic systems are much smaller.

- There is not much difference *between* domestic and regional satellites.

- The ECS system has antennas *very much like* INTELSAT standard antennas.

- Regional satellite systems require that individual countries have their own earth stations, *as with* INTELSAT.
  like

Now express the following ideas using one of the patterns given in the examples above:

- Regional satellite systems cover a small area   = domestic systems

- Regional satellite systems take time to set up   ≠ domestic systems

- Domestic satellite systems do not require that international conferences are held   ≠ regional systems

- Domestic satellite systems use simple receivers on the ground   = regional systems

- Domestic and regional satellites require small receiving antennas   ≠ INTELSAT satellites

2. CONNECTIVES

Notice these two types of words and phrases which are used to connect ideas together in writing and in speech:

Type A   Therefore
             Consequently
             However
             On the other hand
             Moreover
             That is to say
             Indeed
             In this case / in that case

All these are separated from the rest of the sentence by commas.

- There is conceptually not a great deal of difference between a regional satellite system used by a group of neighbouring countries and a domestic system used by a large or dispersed country. *Indeed*, they share a common characteristic which makes them quite different from the INTELSAT system.

- Each INTELSAT satellite must have a beam accessible to roughly one third of the globe . . . *On the other hand*, a circular beam could cover the whole of India if it had a radius on the ground of 1450 km.

- All else being equal, it means that the satellite antenna gain can, *in this case*, be increased by a factor of 26.

Type B   Although
             Since
             As
             Because
             In order for/In order that . . .
             While
             Whereas

These connectives introduce subordinate clauses and should not be followed by commas.

- *Since* stationary satellites present no tracking problems, most operators prefer them.

- *Although* the conceptual difference between a regional and a domestic satellite is not great, the political difference is enormous.

▼

Now choose the best word or phrase to complete each of the following sentences:

- It is difficult to make predictions about technological changes in the future. [However, / Consequently, / Although,] it is possible to get some idea of the changes which might occur.

- When making an international telephone call, the signal may travel a distance of 72,000 km. It is, [moreover, / whereas, / therefore,] not surprising that 600 milliseconds passes between the time you finish speaking and the time when the reply comes back.

- It is expected that the use of submarine cables will prove cheaper than satellites by the mid 1990s. [That is to say, / In this case, / In order that,] it is likely that the number of satellites will be reduced.

- [Although / Indeed / Because] satellites have a high reliability, earth stations are frequently affected by weather and require more maintenance.

- [While / Since / On the other hand] high frequency radio is still used a lot for ship-to-ship communications, many ship-to-shore communications are now conducted via satellites.

- Initially only three satellites were used for maritime communications, [consequently, / that is to say, / because,] one for each ocean region.

- Many countries now have domestic satellite systems using their own satellites. [Moreover, / While, / In this case,] nearly 20 countries operate domestic services by leasing spacecraft capacity from INTELSAT.

- The first domestic satellite system was established in 1969, [therefore / whereas / that is to say] the first regional system did not develop until the mid 1970s.

E. Understanding a lecture

Listen to the lecture and take notes. Then try to answer the questions below.

1. • What is the lecture about?
   • What different communications systems are mentioned in the lecture?
   • Which of these systems has been developed most recently?
   • Which one does the lecturer think will be most important in the future?

2. • How many cables are normally carried in a tube in a major system?
   • How many channels would such a system provide?
   • Is a single cable used to carry transmissions in both directions?

- How many trans-Atlantic cables were in use in 1984?
- What is the diameter of a standard coaxial system?

3. • What are optic fibres made of?
   • What kind of waves are transmitted by optic fibres?
   • How are these waves generated?
   • Why are fibres needed for light transmission?
   • What diameter is given for a standard optic-fibre system?

4. List the four main advantages which optic-fibre systems have over coaxial systems.

F. Understanding a printed text (2)

Read the following text which explains how long distance telephone calls are connected.

15–4.2 Telephone Exchanges (Switches) and Routing

The function of a telephone exchange (switch) is to interconnect four-wire lines, so as to permit a call to be established correctly. If both the calling and the called subscriber are connected to the same exchange, it merely has to interconnect them. If the wanted subscriber is connected to some other exchange, the call from calling subscriber must be routed correctly, so that it will reach the wanted number.

There have been basically three generations of exchanges. The first was the step-by-step, or Strowger type, which had an incredible number of relays that made interconnections step by step, i.e., after each digit was received. The second generation was the *crossbar* exchange, which had even more relays but miniaturized and arranged so that up to 20 connections were made simultaneously by the crossbar switch, after all the digits were received. The *processor-controlled* exchange represents the third generation. Here, all the interconnections are made by the exchange processor or computer, and as a result the space occupied is very much smaller. It is worth pointing out that a telephone (or telex) exchange is an incredibly complex piece of equipment, and a 2000-line crossbar exchange may occupy the whole floor of a rather large building. In countries such as the United States and Australia, there are very few Strowger exchanges left, processor-controlled exchange capacities have outstripped those of crossbar exchanges, and most of the latest exchanges are digital. If the originating and wanted subscribers are not connected to the same exchange, the originating exchange must participate in the correct routing of the call. This is done by analyzing the called number and examining the paths available through and outside the exchange to route the call. The local exchange must establish the group of first-choice trunks to which the call is routed, and which of these is free. If all are occupied, the call is routed to the second-choice trunks, and so on. If no trunks are available, the appropriate signal must be sent to the calling subscriber, in this case perhaps a 'plant engaged' tone. The same process is performed in each exchange in the hierarchy of exchanges, which is essentially local office — toll center — primary or regional center — international center, and then the same chain in reverse.

As an example, let us examine the routing that may be taken by a call from the small town of Daylesford in Victoria (Australia) to New York. The call will be routed to the toll office in Ballarat, directly or via some intermediate point, and then to the regional center in Melbourne. From there it is routed via any one of a number of paths to its opposite number in Sydney, whence it is sent to one of the two international exchanges in Sydney. A Denver–Sydney satellite or cable circuit is then selected, and in Denver the call is routed from the international exchange to a regional one, then perhaps to the New York No. 6 regional office, then to a toll centre, the correct local office and finally to the wanted subscriber. Had all the Denver–Sydney circuits been busy, the Sydney exchange would have selected a Sacramento–Sydney circuit, and the consequent trunk routing to New York would have been different. It is worth noting that the process just described should not take more than a few seconds.

These, then, are some of the functions of telephone exchanges. Others include self-monitoring, the provision of statistical data on traffic and performance, and even customer charging. These topics are discussed in greater detail in [42] and [43].

G. Kennedy. *Electronic Communication Systems*, pp 573–4. McGraw-Hill, 1985.

G. Check your understanding

1. Telephony has many of its own terms which appeared in the text you have just read. Do you know the meaning of these terms? Match the terms (listed in the left-hand column) with the definitions or explanations (listed in the right-hand column).

A. Call	a. Long distance telephone line
B. Calling subscriber	b. Device which receives and transmits messages
C. Called subscriber	c. Office where cost of call is calculated
D. Exchange	d. A telephone interaction
E. Engaged tone	e. Control office where lines are connected
F. Relay	f. Transmission of a call via a particular path
G. Route	g. Person who uses the phone
H. Subscriber	h. Person who places the call
I. Toll centre	i. Person for whom the call is intended
J. Trunk	j. The sound heard on the telephone when the line you want is busy

2. Complete the table with the required data about the different generations of telephone exchange:

Strowger	Crossbar	Processor-controlled
Large number of relays		
	Up to 20 connections made simultaneously after all digits have been received.	
		Occupies much smaller space

3. Label the diagram:

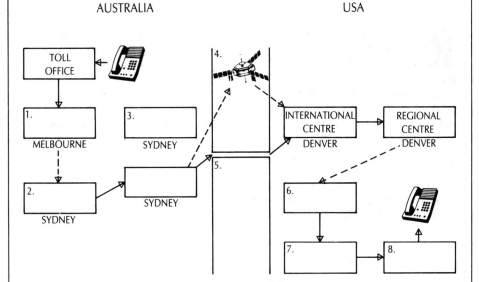

AUSTRALIA   USA

4. Complete the sentences:

- If both calling and called subscribers are connected to the same exchange . . .

- If calling and called subscriber are not connected to the same exchange . . .

- If the first choice of trunk lines are occupied . . .

- If all trunk lines are occupied . . .

H. Understanding discourse

You will hear an international telephone call between two friends, Joe and Ahmed. Listen to the conversation and then answer these questions.

1. What did you learn about the two men making the call? Complete the sentences:

- Ahmed is calling from ....

- Ahmed and Joe haven't seen each other for ....

- They know each other because ....

- Bob Collins was their ....

- Ahmed has finished ...., but Joe won't finish until ....

2. What did you understand about Bob Collins' new invention? Answer the questions:

- What has he built?

- What is this device connected to?

- What must be done to the radio signals before they are fed to this device?

- What does the device do?

- What does Bob Collins hope to achieve with the device?

▼

ENGINEERING DESIGN

A. Understanding a printed text (1)

Read the following text about the **design process**, paying attention to the structure, paragraphing and subheadings.

As you read, look for the answers to the following questions. Remember that you do not have to understand every word to answer the questions.

1. The writer outlines six steps which are normally followed when designing a system. What are they and in what order are they usually followed?

2. Which is the most important step in the design process, according to the writer?

3. Which step demands most inventiveness and creativity?

4. Which step usually involves detailed calculations?

5. What can happen if the design is not properly communicated to the organisation who will use it?

The Design Process

We frequently talk about designing 'a system'. By a system, we mean the entire combination of hardware, information and people necessary to accomplish some specified mission. A system may be an electric power distribution network for a region of the nation, a procedure for detecting flaws in welded pressure vessels, or a combination of production steps to produce automobile parts. A large system usually is divided into subsystems, which in turn are made up of components.

There is no universally acclaimed sequence of steps that leads to a workable design. However, let us more or less arbitrarily consider the process to consist of the following steps:

Recognition of a need
Definition of a problem
Gathering information
Conceptualization
Evaluation
Communication of the design

The design process generally proceeds from top to bottom in the list, but it must be understood that in practice some of the steps will be carried out in parallel and that feedback leading to iteration is a common fact of design.

Recognition of a need

Needs usually arise from dissatisfaction with the existing situation. They may be to reduce cost, increase reliability, or just change because the public has become bored with the product.

Definition of a problem

Probably the most critical step in the design process is the definition of the problem. The true problem is not always what it seems to be at first glance. Because this step requires such a small part of the total time to create the final design, its importance is often overlooked. Figure 2–3 illustrates how the final design can differ greatly depending upon how the problem is defined.

It is advantageous to define the problem as broadly as possible. If the definition is broad, you will be less likely to overlook unusual or unconventional solutions. Broad treatment of problems that previously were attacked in piecemeal fashion can have a big payoff. However, you should realize that the degree to which you can pursue a broad problem formulation toward a final design will depend on factors often outside your control. In most cases, the extent to which you are able to follow a broad problem formulation will depend on the importance of the problem, the limits on time and money that have been placed on the problem and your own position in the organization.

One approach that you should not take is to consider the existing solution to the problem to be the problem itself. That approach immediately submerges you in the trees of the forest, and you will find yourself generating solutions to a problem you have failed to define.

The definition of a problem should include writing down a formal problem statement, which should express as specifically as possible what the design is intended to accomplish. It should include objectives and goals, definitions of any special technical terms, the constraints placed upon the design, and the criteria that will be used to evaluate the design.

Perhaps the best way to proceed is to develop a problem statement at the initial problem definition step and then, in the second iteration after much information has been gathered, develop a much more detailed problem statement that is usually called the problem analysis.

As proposed by the project sponsor   As specified in the project request   As designed by the senior designer

As produced by manufacturing   As installed at the user's site   What the user wanted

Figure 2-3 Note how the design depends on the viewpoint of the individual who defines the problem.

Gathering information

Perhaps the greatest frustration you will encounter when you embark on your first design problem will be due to the dearth or plethora of information. No longer will your responsibility stop with the knowledge contained in a few chapters of a text. Your assigned problem may be in a technical area in which you have no previous background and you will not even have a single basic reference on the subject. At the other extreme you may be presented with a mountain of reports of previous work and your task will be to keep from drowning in paper. Whatever the situation, the immediate task is to identify the needed pieces of information and find or develop that information.

Conceptualization

The conceptualization step is to determine the elements, mechanisms, processes or configurations that in some combination or other result in a design that satisfies the need. It is the key step for employing inventiveness and creativity.

Very often the conceptualization step involves the formulation of a model which may be either of the two general types: analyzed and experimental. A vital aspect of the conceptualization process is synthesis. Synthesis is the process of taking elements of the concept and arranging them in the proper order, sized and dimensioned in the proper way. Synthesis is a creative process and is present in every design.

Design is very individualized. There are no ironclad rules for teaching successful design, and unfortunately very little has been written about the conceptualization step that is at the heart of the design process.

Evaluation

The evaluation step involves a thorough analysis of the design. The term evaluation is used more in the sense of weighing and judging than in the sense of grading. Typically, the evaluation step may involve detailed calculation, often computer calculation, of the performance of the design by using an analytical model. In other cases, the evaluation may involve extensive simulated service testing of an experimental model or perhaps a full-sized prototype.

Communication of the design

It must always be kept in mind that the purpose of the design is to satisfy the needs of a client or customer. Therefore, the finalized design must be properly communicated or it may lose much of its impact or significance. The communication is usually by oral presentation to the sponsor as well as by a written design report. Detailed engineering drawings, computer programs and working models are frequently part of the 'deliverables' to the customer. It hardly needs to be emphasized that communication is not a one-time thing to be carried out at the end of the project. In a well-run design project, there is continual oral and written dialog between the project manager and the customer.

G. Dieter. *Engineering Design*, pp 32–34. McGraw-Hill, 1983.

B. Check your understanding

Now read the text again carefully. While you read, look for the answers to these questions:

1. Select the item that best completes each of these sentences:

● A system . . .
(a) is the result of a design process.
(b) is made up of a sequence of steps.
(c) means the equipment needed to do a job.
(d) may or may not need people.

● The writer recommends that design engineers should . . .
(a) define the problem as broadly as possible.
(b) attack a problem in piecemeal fashion.
(c) use the existing solution as a starting point.
(d) not spend too much time on defining the problem.

● The problem statement should . . .
(a) be considered only after all the information has been gathered.
(b) be as detailed as possible.
(c) express specifically the objectives of the final design.
(d) be written in the form of a series of questions.

● The conceptualisation step . . .
(a) has been described in detail in many books on design.
(b) must be carried out in accordance with specific rules.
(c) involves rearranging the basic concepts in the proper way.
(d) is approached in the same way by all design engineers.

2. In the following, mark all the items which you think are FALSE:

● A need for a new design can arise when the existing design . . .
(a) is too expensive. ☐
(b) doesn't work reliably. ☐
(c) has been around a long time. ☐
(d) is boring. ☐

● The difficulties of gathering information for a new design are:
(a) you may not have any previous experience of the subject. ☐
(b) you may not know which textbook to refer to. ☐
(c) there may be too much information. ☐
(d) there may not be anything written on the subject. ☐

● The following factors are important for the success of the final design:
(a) The design must be fully analysed with reference to an analytical model, experimental model or prototype. ☐
(b) The qualities of the design must be observed. ☐
(c) Interaction with the sponsor or client while the design process is going on. ☐
(d) The sponsor or client must be told what to expect. ☐
(e) Effective communication by means of drawings, written reports, oral presentations, demonstrations etc. ☐

3. The writer uses a number of unusual words and phrases. See if you can work out the meaning of them from the context, and express the meaning in your own words.

- to accomplish a specified mission
- universally acclaimed
- iteration
- in piecemeal fashion
- a big payoff
- dearth and plethora of information
- ironclad rules

C. Increase your vocabulary

Remember that you can use a dictionary to help you answer these questions.

1. Find words in the text which mean the following:

- what you are aiming to achieve with a design
- the lack of something or requirement for something
- something which restricts what you can do
- standards by which something can be judged
- the impression made by an idea

2. Which of the following adjectives fits best into each of the sentences below?

- critical
- finalised
- unconventional
- workable

- We could discuss your idea and if it seems to be ...., we could plan the evaluation stage.

- The next stage of the project is .... If it fails, everything else fails.

- Some of his designs are very .... They are not what most people would expect, but they do work.

- When everything is ...., we must prepare the presentation and report for our sponsors.

3. Match each of the verbs below with the phrase which best goes with it:

- Accomplish .... solutions to a problem
- Proceed .... a new idea
- Carry out .... the needs of a client
- Create .... a task
- Generate .... research or test work
- Formulate .... from step to step
- Satisfy .... someone to a project
- Assign .... a problem in precise terms

D. Check your grammar

1. MODALS OF OBLIGATION

Required	*Not prohibited*
must	may
should	can
have to	could
need to	

Not required	*Prohibited*
do not have to	should not
need not	must not
	may not

Examples: You *must* meet all specified requirements.
You *should* define the problem as broadly as possible.
You *may* approach the problem in any way you wish.
We *need to* analyse the problem before we can solve it.

These steps *need not* be carried out in a specific order.
You *should not* consider the existing solution to be the problem itself.
The cost *must not* exceed $5 million.
may not

Now complete the following sentences with the appropriate modal verb. Note that some answers will be negative.

- This data is confidential. It _____ reach the ears of anyone outside this office.

- I think we _____ decide how urgently we need this equipment before we make a commitment to buy it.

- The materials used for molten metal ladles _____ be capable of withstanding very high temperatures.

- The material used for lining refrigerators _____ to withstand very high temperatures.

- The reactions of chemical substances _____ be represented by chemical equations that show the formulae and relative numbers of the reactants or products involved.

- You _____ tell me. I have read about it already!

- You _____ borrow my technical dictionary if you want.

- You _____ write up the results of the tests very carefully.

2. HYPOTHESISING

When we consider the results of different possible solutions to a problem, we normally use the *second conditional*.

Examples:

- Increase thickness ... steel plate stronger.

If we increased the thickness, the steel plate *would be* stronger.

- Select stronger material ... losses minimised

If we selected a stronger material, our losses *would be* minimised.

Now write the following notes into similar sentences:

- Use hot rolling method … production costs reduced
- Use hot rolling method … less chance of cracking
- Minimise size of furnace openings … air leakages prevented
- Use exhaust gases for heating … save energy costs
- Fabrication includes welding … weldable grade of steel needed
- A fire starts … alarm activated by smoke detectors

3. HYPOTHETICAL STATEMENTS

> When we are describing a hypothetical situation, it is not necessary to continue to specify 'If this was the case' or 'If this solution was carried out'. It is often understood. However, we must continue to use the modal verb 'would':
>
> Example: If this new technology were developed . . .
>
> . . . there *would be* many advantages for the local people. Jobs *would be created* and there *would be* greater prosperity. However, the initial investment costs would be high, and that *would have to be* taken into consideration.

Now expand the following notes into two short paragraphs:

A new way of treating organic wastes invented; uses a column of fluidised sand. Dairy farmers able to use this system to treat their milk wastes. — Save some of their costs. No longer need to pay water authorities for drainage facilities. Instead, able to use waste as valuable fertiliser.

Growing concern about increase of carbon dioxide in the atmosphere. Thought that this increase could lead to a rise in world average temperatures. Then, polar ice melt; ocean levels rise; many major cities (e.g. London) flood; drought in many parts of the world; food production affected.

E. Understanding a lecture

In this lecture, you will hear about an example of a design problem, and how it can be analysed. The lecture has been divided into four sections to help you to follow it. Listen for the answers to the following questions:

Section 1

1. What is wrong with the problem as it is stated in this section?
2. What must be done before the problem statement can be completed?
3. Label Figure 2–5, below.

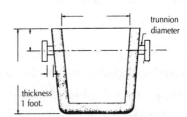

trunnion diameter

thickness 1 foot.

Figure 2–5 Details of ladle used for design.

1. What is the ladle made of?
2. What is the capacity of the ladle? (What weight of molten metal can it hold?)
3. What are the maximum temperatures which the ladle will have to withstand?
4. What other conditions of service are mentioned which are important to consider in the design of the ladle hooks?
5. What are the essential qualities which the design must have?

Section 3

1. Label Figure 2–6.

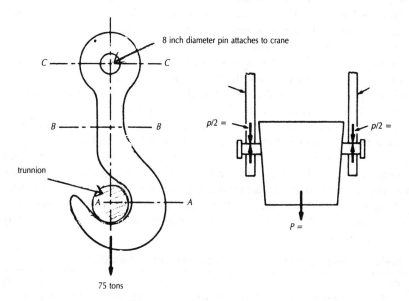

8 inch diameter pin attaches to crane

C — · — · — C

B — · — · — B

trunnion

A — · — A

$p/2 =$ $p/2 =$

$P =$

75 tons

Figure 2–6 Details of ladle hook and ladle

2. Match the name of each part of the hook with the three critical stress regions: A, B and C:

A   Shank of the hook
B   Bight of the hook
C   Eye of the hook

3. What three dimensions need to be established from the calculation of stresses in each region?

F. Understanding a printed text (2)

The following text continues with the problem already discussed in the lecture in Section E. Now you can read about the decisions made concerning materials and dimensions of the ladle hooks.

Material selection and working stress

It is almost axiomatic that a load-bearing member 8 to 10 ft tall, in a situation where dead weight is not critical, will be made from steel.

Cost and reliability of the product are the chief considerations in selecting the method for manufacturing the ladle hook. The prime decision is whether to use a monolithic hook with the 7.1 in thickness produced by forging or casting or to build up the thickness from several layers of hot-rolled steel plate. The latter method was chosen because it is cheaper than forging or casting when production lots are relatively small. Also, in thickness of less than 1½ in, hot-rolled steel plate has relatively uniform and predictable mechanical properties. In addition, the laminated hook provides a redundant structure. Should one of the plates develop a fatigue crack or fail from brittle fracture, the fracture will not propagate immediately to all of the plates. Thus, there should be time to locate the crack during a routine inspection and repair the hook.

Therefore, we need to make a selection from the standard grades of carbon- and low-alloy-steel plates that are commercially available.

Structural-quality steel plate is designated by various ASTM specifications. Steels of this type fall into three categories: 1) plain hot-rolled carbon steels, 2) high-strength low-alloy steel (HSLA) in which grain refiners have been added to control the hot-rolled grain size, and 3) alloy steels which are quenched and tempered for high strength. Since welding may be used in fabrication, only weldable grades with less than 0.30 percent carbon will be considered. The A36 has impact and brittle fracture characteristics that make it unsatisfactory for this application.

Table 2–1 Characteristics of candidate structural steels*

ASTM spec.	Description	C	Mn	Other	YS, psi	UTS, psi	Relative cost
A36	Carbon steel	0.29	1.0	8	36,000	60,000	1.0
A441	HSLA steel	0.22	1.25	0.02 V	50,000	70,000	1.15
A242	HSLA steel	0.15	1.10	0.05 V, 0.3 Cu	50,000	70,000	1.25
A514	Alloy steel	0.15	0.80	Ni-Cr-Mo	100,000	120,000	2.0

*'Metals Handbook', 9th ed., pp. 181–190, American Society for Metals, Metals Park, Ohio, 1978.

Let's say that the detailed stress analysis has produced the following dimensions:

thickness of steel plate structure,	t = 7.1 inches
width of shank	w = 6 inches
dimensions of eye	a = 6.2 inches
(see diagram)	b = 8 inches
bight section,	c = 24 inches
(see diagram)	

Final dimensions

These dimensions have been based on keeping the nominal stresses at a level below 12,500 psi. At this point the ladle hook should be drawn to scale to check the validity of the calculated dimensions and establish the remaining dimensions. Some of the latter will be set by functional requirements; others will be set by engineering common sense. For example, the distance between the crane pin and the trunnion must be great enough to accommodate one-half the width of the ladle if it is tipped to its maximum extent.

When drawn to scale, the overall dimensions of the hook look awkward, Fig. 2–8a. The width of the shank looks far too narrow for the eye and the bight section. Also, the widest bight section looks too wide.

Since the hook is cut from steel plate, we realize there is little extra cost (except for extra weight) if the width at the shank is increased from 6 to 12 in. This permits an easier transition section with the eye and results in a much less fragile looking design.

The width at the bight section can be reduced by increasing the thickness. Decreasing from 24 to 18 in requires an increase in thickness from $t = 7.1$ to $t = 9.6$ in. This is more costly because it requires more steel plates in the final hook. However, it has the advantage of producing a more stable hook in that the centre of gravity at the hook now coincides with the centerline through the eye and the trunnion.

G. Dieter. *Engineering Design*, pp 50–52. McGraw-Hill, 1983.

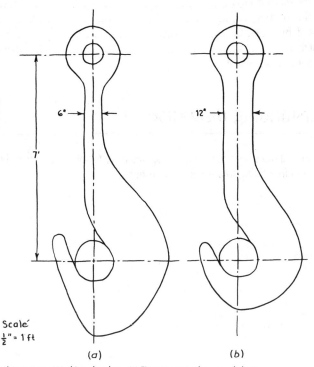

Scale
$\frac{1}{2}" = 1\,ft$

(a)   (b)

Figure 2–8 Working sketches. *(a)* First attempt; *(b)* second design.

G. Check your understanding

1. Complete the sentences:

- A steel plate structure is preferable to a cast or forged steel body mainly because ....
- Steel plate also has .... properties.
- If a fatigue crack occurs in one of the steel plates, the crack or fracture ....
- Only grades of steel which are weldable are considered because ....
- The A36 cannot be considered because ....

Now refer to Table 2–1 and see if you can complete these sentences:

- The A514 is not suitable because ....
- The A242 has an advantage over the A441 in that ....
- A441 was chosen as the best material for the ladle hooks because ....

2. Answer these questions:

- How is the validity of the calculated dimensions checked?
- What two factors determine the remaining dimensions?
- How is the distance between the crane pin and the trunnion calculated?

3. Refer to Figure 2–8 in the text and complete these sentences comparing the left-hand
design (a) with the one on the right (b):

- The width of the shank in (a) is .... than (b).
- The bight section of (a) is .... than (b).
- The thickness of (b) is .... than (a).
- The design of (b) is .... than that of (a).
- The disadvantage of (b) is that it is .... than (a).

H. Understanding discourse

You will hear a formal discussion in which four speakers try to solve a problem. Listen to the
whole discussion before trying to answer the questions.

1. What is the decision which the speakers have to make?

2. Look at the decision tree diagram below, and complete the labels 1–8.

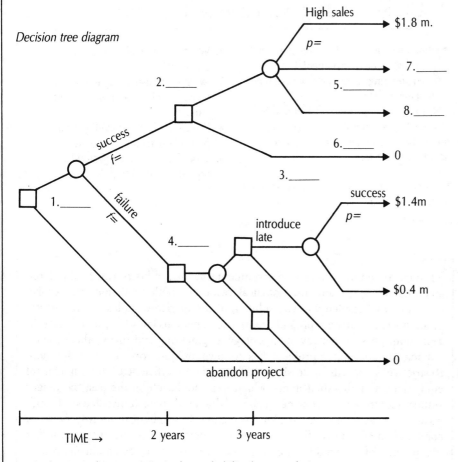

Decision tree diagram

High sales

$1.8 m.

p=

2._____

7._____

5._____

8._____

6._____

0

3._____

success

f=

success

$1.4m

p=

introduce
late

1._____

failure

f=

4._____

$0.4 m

0

abandon project

TIME →   2 years   3 years

3. In the same diagram, write in the probability factor each time you see p=

4. What decision do you think the group was about to make?

ENGINEERING AND THE EARTH'S RESOURCES

A. Understanding a printed text (1)

The following text discusses some of the problems of **environmental engineering**, with particular reference to the United States.

Read the passage through and find the answers to these questions. Remember, you do not have to understand every word to answer the questions.

1. How are air pollutants generally treated? Name four different processes referred to in the text.

2. What are the main causes of air pollution?

3. What is the usual way to control emissions of gas and particles into the atmosphere?

4. Which gas is mentioned as being particularly difficult to control?

5. What industries are affected by regulations to control the emission of this gas?

Through its interdisciplinary environmental teams, industry is directing large amounts of capital and technological resources both to define and resolve environmental challenges. The solution of the myriad complex environmental problems requires the skills and experience of persons knowledgeable in health, sanitation, physics, biology, meteorology, engineering and many other fields.

Each air and water problem has its own unique approach and solution. Restrictive standards necessitate high retention efficiencies for all control equipment. Off-the-shelf items, which were applicable in the past, no longer suffice. Controls must now be specifically tailored to each installation. Liquid wastes can generally be treated by chemical or physical means, or by a combination of the two, for removal of contaminants with the expectation that the majority of the liquid can be recycled. Air or gaseous contaminants can be removed by scrubbing, filtration, absorption or adsorption and the clean gas discharged into the atmosphere. The removed contaminants, either dry or in solution, must be handled wisely, or a new water- or air-pollution problem may result.

Industries that extract natural resources from the earth, and in so doing disturb the surface, are being called upon to reclaim and restore the land to a condition and contour that is equal to or better than the original state.

Air quality management. The air contaminants which pervade the environment are many and emanate from multiple sources. A sizeable portion of these contaminants are produced by nature. The greatest burden of atmospheric pollutants resulting from human activity comprises carbon monoxides, hydrocarbons, particulates, sulfur oxides and nitrogen oxides, in that order. About 50% of the major pollutants in the United States come from the use of the internal combustion engine.

Industrial and fuel combustion sources (primarily utility power plants) together contribute approximately 30% of the major pollutants.

The general trend in gaseous and particulate control is to limit the emissions from a process stack to a specified weight per hour based on the total material weight processed to assure compliance with ambient air regulation. Process weights become extremely large in steel and cement plants and in large nonferrous smelters. The degree of control necessary in such plants can approach 100% of all particulate matter in the stack. Retention equipment can become massive both in physical size and in cost. The equipment may include high-energy venturi scrubbers, fabric arresters, and electrostatic precipitators. Each application must be evaluated so that the selected equipment will provide the retention efficiency desired.

Sulfur oxide retention and control present the greatest challenges to industrial environmental engineers. Ambient air standards are extremely low and the emission standards calculated to meet these ambient standards place an enormous challenge on the affected industries. Many copper smelters and all coal-fired utility power plants have large volume, weak-sulfur-dioxide effluent gas streams. Scrubbing these weak-sulfur-dioxide gas streams with limestone slurries or caustic solutions is extremely expensive, requires prohibitively large equipment, and creates water and solid waste disposal problems of enormous magnitude. Installations employing dry scrubbing have been used on very low-sulfur-dioxide gas streams.

Copper smelters are required to remove 85–90% of the sulfur contained in the feed concentrate. Smelters using the old-type reverbatory furnaces produce large volumes of gas containing low concentrations of sulfur dioxide which is not amenable to removal by acid making. However, gas streams from newer-type flash and roaster-electric furnace operations can produce low-volume gas streams containing more than 4% sulfur dioxide which can be treated more economically to obtain elemental sulfur, liquid sulfur dioxide, or sulfuric acid. Smelters generally have not considered the scrubbing of weak-sulfur-dioxide gas streams as a viable means of attaining emission limitations because of the tremendous quantities of solid wastes that would be generated.

The task of upgrading weak smelter gas streams to produce products which have no existing market has led to extensive research into other methods of producing copper. A number of mining companies piloted, and some have constructed, hydrometallurgical plants to produce electrolytic-grade copper from ores by chemical means, thus eliminating the smelting step. These plants have generally experienced higher unit costs than smelters and a number have been plagued with operational problems. It does not appear likely that hydrometallurgical plants will replace conventional smelting in the foreseeable future. Liquid ion exchange followed by electrowinning, is also being used more extensively for the heap leaching of low-grade copper. This method produces a very pure grade of copper without the emission of sulfur dioxide to the atmosphere.

S.P. Parker (Ed.) *Encyclopedia of Environmental Science*. McGraw-Hill

B. Check your understanding

Read the text again carefully. While you read it, look for the answers to these questions:

1. Are these statements True or False?

- Environmental problems require the expertise of people with differing scientific backgrounds. ☐

- There are many devices on the market which can be used to solve all kinds of air and water problems. ☐

- Liquid wastes can be largely recycled after treatment. ☐

- Mining and quarrying industries are no longer allowed to leave the land surface in a disturbed condition. ☐

- The highest proportion of atmospheric pollutants produced by man comprises carbon monoxides. ☐

- 30% of air pollutants have natural causes. ☐

- Regulations are concerned with emissions into the atmosphere of gases rather than solids. ☐

- Limestone slurries and caustic solutions are used to control sulphur oxide gas emissions. ☐

- Useful by-products can be obtained by treating gas streams from modern copper smelting operations. ☐

- New methods of producing copper by chemical means have been highly successful. ☐

2. Classify the following items into *four* lists according to their role in environmental engineering. Then find a heading for each list.

electrolytic grade copper	liquid sulphur dioxide
electrostatic precipitator	hydrocarbons
electrowinning	hydrometallurgical plant
fabric arrester	nitrogen oxide gases
flash furnace	sulphur dioxide gas
liquid ion exchange	sulphuric acid

3. Discussion.

- Why do you think air quality management is important?

- What kinds of air pollution are found in your area? What could be done to control them?

C. Increase your vocabulary

In this section, you should use your dictionary to help you answer the questions about the text.

1. Distinguishing between words of similar meaning. Insert one of the following words in each sentence as appropriate.

- effluent ● disposal ● discharge ● extracted ● emanated

- The safe _____ of waste products is often a problem for industry.

- The _____ of water from a reservoir must be carefully controlled.

- There is a steady flow of _____ from the sewage works into the sea.

- An unpleasant smell _____ from the factory.

- Copper concentrate is _____ from ore and is then smelted and refined.

2. Match each of the words in the list with the definition which best goes with it.

● retain	....	have somebody obey a rule or standard
● restrict	....	put back in its original place
● regulate	....	bring back to its original state; rebuild
● reclaim	....	bring back to a useful condition
● restore	....	keep hold of; prevent from being released
● replace	....	keep within certain limits

3. There are a number of words and phrases in the text which refer to the *large size* of things. Find as many as you can and make a list.

D. Check your grammar

1. NUMBER, AMOUNT AND PROPORTION

Do you remember?

	Uncountable things	Countable things
●	all	all
◖	much, a lot of a great deal of a large amount of	many, a lot of the majority of a large number of
◓	some a portion of a proportion of	some a number of several
◔	a little (of)/not much a small part of hardly any	few (a few of)/not many a small number of a minority (of)

Examples:

- *There are many* contaminants in the atmosphere. *A great deal of* money is being spent on solving environmental problems.

- *A number of* mining companies have piloted hydrometallurgical plants.

- *Very little* waste is allowed to escape into the atmosphere. *Few* people understand the difficulties in reducing sulphur dioxide emissions.

Now write the appropriate word or phrase into each of the following sentences:

- A company is reponsible for the health, safety and care of ● its employees.

- ◐ accidents can be prevented if ◔ precautions are taken.

- If there are ◕ injuries, ◕ working time is lost.

- ◔ people believe there should be more regulations to control the environment.

- The mining industry causes ◔ damage to the environment.

2. VERB TENSES

Notice the use of verb tenses in relation to TIME as shown in the diagram.

In 1965, the first geostationary satellite *was launched*.

Coal-fired power plants still *produce* contaminants.

Before the 1960s, satellite transmission of TV *had not been achieved*.

NOW

We *have made* a lot of progress in improving the environment.

There *will be* a greater need for energy in the future.

PAST ────────────────────────────→ FUTURE

During the sixties, Americans *were working* hard to put a man on the moon.

We *are developing* new techniques for reducing air pollution.

Now write the verbs in the sentences below in the correct form:

- Two hours ago, an accident _____ (occur) at the Goldberg mine.

- Miners _____ (blast) the rock with explosives, but not all the explosives _____ (detonate).

- As a result, one miner _____ (kill) and two others _____ (trap) underground.

- Rescue teams _____ (work) hard to dig the miners out, but so far they _____ (not, succeed) in reaching the trapped miners.

- A spokesman from the mine said: "We hope that the men _____ (bring) to safety in a few hours."

- He said that an accident of this seriousness _____ (happen, never) before at the Goldberg mine.

- A full investigation _____ (carry out) to discover why the explosives _____ (fail).

E. Understanding a lecture

Listen to the lecture, which has been divided into three sections, and then answer the questions below.

1.
- This lecture is one in a series. What is the series about?

- What is the lecture about?

- Find a suitable sub-heading for each of the three sections.

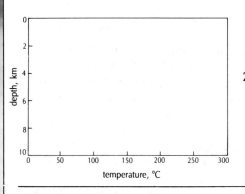

2. This graph is referred to in Section 1 of the lecture as Graph 1. Draw the curve of the graph according to the description given in the lecture.

---

3. These questions refer to Section 2 of the lecture.

- The terms *porous* and *permeability* are used to describe the rock where natural geothermal reservoirs are found. Define the two terms.

- Thermal energy is obtained from underground rocks by ....

- Are natural geothermal reservoirs . . .
  - (a) found everywhere? ☐
  - (b) fairly common? ☐
  - (c) not so common? ☐
  - (d) rare? ☐

- What are the four conditions which must be met if a source of geothermal energy is to be made economically viable?

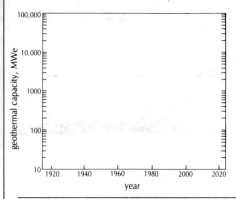

4. This graph is referred to in Section 3 of the lecture as Graph 2. Draw the curve of the graph according to the description given.

---

5. Discussion.

Could geothermal energy solve some of our energy problems in the future?

F. Understanding a printed text (2)

Read the following text about **marine mining**.

Marine Mining is the term used to describe the process of recovering mineral wealth from sea water and from deposits on and under the sea floor. Unknown except to technical specialists before 1960, undersea mining is receiving increasing attention.

There are sound reasons for this sudden emphasis on a previously little-known source of minerals. While the world's demand for mineral commodities is increasing at an alarming rate, most of the developed countries have been thoroughly explored for surface outcroppings of mineral deposits. The mining industry has been required to advance its capabilities for the exploration and exploitation of low-grade and unconventional sources of ore. Corresponding advances in oceanology have highlighted the importance of the ocean as a source of minerals and indicated that the technology required for their exploitation is in some cases already available.

Mining of consolidated deposits Production from consolidated mineral deposits under the sea is already substantial. Undersea coal already accounts for almost 30% of the total coal production in Japan and just less than 10% in Great Britain.

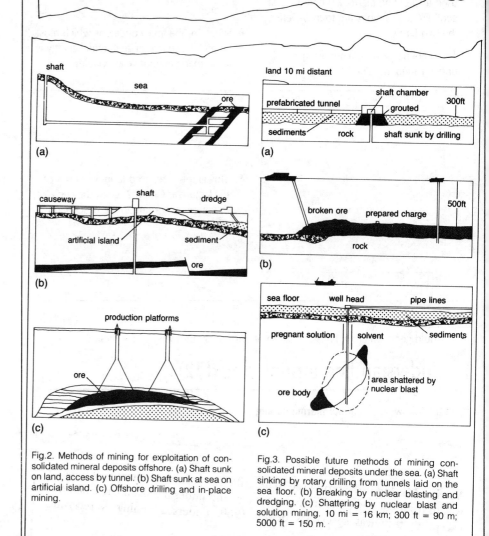

Fig.2. Methods of mining for exploitation of consolidated mineral deposits offshore. (a) Shaft sunk on land, access by tunnel. (b) Shaft sunk at sea on artificial island. (c) Offshore drilling and in-place mining.

Fig.3. Possible future methods of mining consolidated mineral deposits under the sea. (a) Shaft sinking by rotary drilling from tunnels laid on the sea floor. (b) Breaking by nuclear blasting and dredging. (c) Shattering by nuclear blast and solution mining. 10 mi = 16 km; 300 ft = 90 m; 5000 ft = 150 m.

Some of the mining methods are illustrated in Fig. 2. For most of the bedded deposits which extend from shore workings a shaft is sunk on land with access under the sea by tunnel. Massive and vein deposits are also worked in this manner. Normal mining methods are used but precautions must be taken with regard to overhead cover. Near land and in shallow water a shaft is sunk at sea on an artificial island. The islands are constructed by dredging from the seabed or by transporting fill over causeways. Sinking through the island is accompanied by normal precautions for loose, water-logged ground, and development and mining thereafter conventional. The same method is also used in oil drilling. Offshore drilling and in-place mining are used only in the mining of sulfur, but this method has considerable possibilities for the mining of other minerals for which leaching is applicable. Petroleum drilling techniques are used throughout, employing stationary platforms constructed on piles driven into the sea floor or floating drill rigs.

The future Consolidated deposits may call for a variety of new mining methods which will be dependent on the type, grade and chemistry of the deposit, the distance from the land, and the depth of water. Some of these methods are illustrated in Fig. 3. The possibility of direct sea floor access at remote sites through shafts drilled in the sea floor has already been given consideration and will be directly applicable to some undersea mining operations. In relatively shallow water, shafts could be sunk by rotary drilling with caissons. In deeper water the drilling equipment could be placed on the sea floor and the shaft collared on completion. The laying of large diameter undersea pipelines has been accomplished over distances of 25 miles (40 km) and has been planned for greater distances. Subestuarine road tunnels have been built by employing pre-fabricated sections. The sinking of shafts in the sea floor from the extremities of such tunnels should be technically feasible under certain conditions.

Submarine ore bodies of massive dimensions and shallow cover could be broken by means of nuclear charges placed in drill holes. The resulting broken rock could then be removed by dredging. Shattering by nuclear blast and solution mining is a method applicable in any depth of water. This method calls for the contained detonation of a nuclear explosive in the ore body, followed by chemical leaching of the valuable mineral.

There are many other activities which may have a direct bearing on the advancement of undersea mining technology but possibly none as much as the International Decade of Ocean Exploration. The discovery of new deposits brings with it new incentives to overcome the multitude of problems encountered in marine mining.

S.P. Parker (Ed.) *Encyclopedia of Environmental Science*. McGraw-Hill

G. Check your understanding

1. Three reasons are given for the 'sudden emphasis on a previously little-known source of minerals'. What are these reasons?

2. Three methods are given for the mining of consolidated deposits. Use the diagrams in Fig. 2 and practise explaining how each method is carried out.

3. In Fig. 3, possible future methods of undersea mining are illustrated by the three diagrams.

- Mark the sentences in the last three paragraphs of the text which refer to each method. Label the sections you have marked: (a), (b) and (c).

- Tick the items in the sentences below which describe technology already being used at the time the article was written.

(a) Laying of large-diameter undersea pipelines over distances of 40 km or more.
(b) Building road tunnels by means of pre-fabricated sections.
(c) Sinking shafts in the sea bed from the extremities of undersea tunnels.
(d) Drilling shafts in the sea bed.
(e) Breaking up of submarine orebodies by nuclear blast.
(f) Removal of rock by dredging.
(g) Offshore drilling and in-place mining for the mining of minerals other than sulphur.
(h) Extraction of minerals by chemical leaching.

H. Understanding discourse

Listen to the interview with a senior research engineer called Dr Michael Blomberg. Dr Blomberg gives his opinions on future trends in science and technology.

1. What predictions does Dr Blomberg make about technological progress? Make a list.

2. Now classify these predictions in three columns according to how strongly Dr Blomberg expresses his belief that they will happen.

STRONG BELIEF	BELIEF (not strongly held)	UNCERTAIN (it could happen)

3. What questions does the interviewer put to Dr Blomberg?

4. Now prepare three questions that you would ask Dr Blomberg if you were present at the interview.

5. Do you agree with Dr Blomberg's ideas? Say what developments you foresee in science and technology over the next fifty years.